Alannah Conway is born in Monkstown, Co Dublin, her family came to live in Britain when she was very young officially obtaining British Citizenship.

Her business career was finance evolving from retail management, local and central government, a finance company and a major corporate high street bank.

Alannah's writing career began with a short book about her local church for a fund-raising project.

She set up her own career coaching business in the West Midlands, and for a period, was a feature writer for a local magazine *Village Life*. A book followed 'Truework', are you? a complication of weekly blogs.

Dedicated to my late father, Richard, my hero. To my mother Elizabeth, my rock. Each offering inspiration and courage. They taught me the art of justice and fairness.

Alannah Conway

DON'T PUSH ME OUT

AUSTIN MACAULEY PUBLISHERS™

LONDON * CAMBRIDGE * NEW YORK * SHARJAH

A CIP catalogue record for this title is available from the British Library.

ISBN 9781398458093 (Paperback)
ISBN 9781398458109 (ePub e-book)

www.austinmacauley.com

First Published 2023
Austin Macauley Publishers Ltd®
1 Canada Square
Canary Wharf
London
E14 5AA

Mrs Amanda Weakford, Bright VA Typing Services, Surrey

Table of Contents

Our lives in their hands to be destroyed or nurtured, such is the power of
those in authority
Power can be used for the good or used for the bad...
In business, it is mostly used to the bad, or so it appears.

Introduction

It was with great interest that I read about the findings of the Banking Investigation Commission in England. Truly, the scale of the wrongdoings by the banks was epic. They were guilty of fixing the Libor exchange rate, rigging the foreign exchanges, and money laundering, amongst other things. The hidden scandal was the treatment of staff within RB and other corporate institutions. Until now it has remained hidden from public view.

"If it ever got out how a member of staff had been treated, then some people would be taken out and shot!" Words of a senior manager.

This story is about how discrimination and jealousy can overtake common sense and humanitarian beliefs. What was allowed to rule was people's prejudices, power struggles and one-upmanship regardless of business ethics.

"Irish people have an enormous impact on Britain" – TV presenter Ryan Tubridy. Did you know that Winston Churchill's spin doctor was an Irishman? Did you know that an Irish guy shot down more German planes for Britain in World War Two than anyone else!

Gerry Adams regrets the Irish were 'understandable' targets of the troubles and the backlash in Britain. Irish Post, dated 26th October 2013.

The Irish Post-dated the 18th May 2013, an article written by Fiona Audley based on the findings of a researcher/lecturer at the University of Liverpool: "Muslim and Irish communities in Britain are similarly cast as 'suspect communities'. Anti-Irish racism is still a problem, still incidences, still stereotyped, jokes still made, still the chance that when they go to interviews discriminated against due to their Irish accents." The article continues, "The Irish are treated like they are all sympathisers with the IRA or taking part in terrorist activities. Both communities tarnished by the minorities of their fringe extremes."

Following the Birmingham Pub Bombings in November 1974, anti-Irish feelings rose into hatred and showed by 'Irish out of Britain' demonstration marches.

It appears that Margaret Thatcher threw all the Irish into the one pot as being a nation of liars! For an intelligent and educated woman, she had her prejudices!

At the state banquet at Windsor Castle for the visiting President of Ireland, Michael D. Higgins, in April 2014, Her Majesty Queen Elizabeth stated, "Over the years, many Irish migrants to Britain encountered discrimination and a lack of appreciation."

"What gives us the right to play God with people's lives?" Civil Service HEO said to a team manager, Melanie, when it was discovered that she had altered a person's gradings to lower ones.

"Management treats nice people with suspicion!"

"Why did I receive unjust treatment from my employer? What happened to Duty of Care as standard from an employer?"

The story escalates to the rules and regulations being broken on countless levels…

I Am Me!

I was born in Monkstown, Co Dublin, a trendy suburb just outside Dun Laoghaire, a beautiful seaport. I have beautiful memories of my childhood there, however short, because Birmingham, England was to become my home at the age of four.

So, life continued and I was educated at a local Catholic primary school, then followed the path to a private girls' convent school. I have fond and close connections to my Irish roots, both the culture and my own heritage. I am extremely proud to be a member of a distinguished Irish legal family, comprising of an Attorney-General for Ireland, who was famous for the formation of the Irish Constitution. Other family members include Supreme Court Judges, District Attorneys, Barristers and Solicitors. It has been rumoured that we are related to Her Serene Highness, Grace Kelly of Monaco. It is a question I had been asked many times, partly due to having blonde hair, a slim figure, good deportment and I dressed well. But probably more importantly, I was always regarded as a lady, or as someone once said, cultured.

England is my home, with British Citizenship to prove my claim. I am loyal to the British monarchy, compiled scrapbooks covering royal jubilees and royal weddings, and I hasten to add I would not part with them.

Have you ever wondered what your life would have been like if you had taken a different career path? Working for a different company or organisation, meeting different people.

Clive Good worth states, "One very good way for a company to lose money, leave mud on its own reputation, bruise the lives of umpteen people is to make a pig's ear of its own recruitment selection procedures." Oh, how true! Recruit the wrong calibre of people, then internal disorder looms and corruption erodes and spreads like fire. Lost are the people that are honest, just and fair-minded, overpowered by individuals with egos bigger than divas, strutting their walk around the office. Begging for attention from their fellow colleagues by raising their voices higher than required, with the words 'absolutely' and 'we should meet up, old chap' ringing throughout the open-plan office…a deal done.

I went to work for what I regarded as a reputable employer, an international business in the banking sector. I believed it was a chance for success, to obtain achievements, to be acknowledged, to be a member of a team.

I arrived for the interview at the office in Solihull, based in the West Midlands. I was feeling good, the sun was out in all its glory on an August day. I was delighted to be asked to attend for an interview, although the agency had said that there was no doubt I would be interviewed because of my vast experience. I was feeling good because I was eager to place my notice of leaving in the hands of my current manager at a local finance company. The company had difficulty retaining staff due to its bullish attitude toward its customers. It may be a surprise but seven people left the company during the week I left. The Managing Director slammed his door when he got the news I was leaving!

However, let me go back to that glorious day in August 2002. I parked the car, crossed the road, checked that I was not dishevelled, hair still in place, skirt straight and blouse crisp. I was greeted by a friendly receptionist called Barbara who politely told me to take a seat in the reception area. While I waited, it allowed me the time to observe the surroundings, the array of pictures on the walls, consisting of a variety of vehicles taken at various angles, and abstract art. People-viewing makes for an interesting way of passing the time and of course, it can reveal a glimpse behind the façade of a business. Staff went to and fro about their business, some looking more professional than others. Suddenly, I received a cheerful 'good morning' and a pleasant smile from a foreign gentleman. I acknowledged the greeting. Of course, later I was to discover that it was the Chief Executive. Overall, what I saw and more importantly felt was that there was a pleasant working atmosphere.

Time for the interview, I was greeted by a smartly dressed blonde lady, her name was Melanie. She explained how she had been 'poached' by one of the directors. Apparently, she had been employed by a competitor. The interview went well, and I secured a job as senior credit controller within the Vehicle Management division of the Royal Bank.

My New Day

The morning of the 13th September 2001 soon arrived and I entered my new place of work relaxed in the knowledge that all was going to be good. After all, it was a major employer. Melanie had said that after three months probationary period, rather than the usual six months, I would be made permanent. So, it was going to be a nice Christmas present for me.

After the staff introductions, I was shown to my desk. It was next to Elaine, a friendly, open person with a good sense of humour. I was put in control of the Public Sector ledger due to my knowledge of central and local government. The Credit Control department had its own room with bars on the windows. The joke was that it was to keep the Rottweilers in not out!

We were a mixed group, with mixed ages, experience and knowledge, but we all got on very well with each other. I duly worked hard and got three years' backlog cleared left by the previous 'owner' of the ledger. All was well, I was getting glowing feedback…onwards and upwards.

Melanie was good to work for. Carol and Lesley, the team leaders, were easy to approach. Lesley and I became good friends. We discovered that Melanie had only worked at RB since August and was feeling her way. She praised and encouraged everyone to succeed.

Like a hurricane developing, the atmosphere changed around us. Why I don't know. Mark, who sat on the other side of me, was complaining about the sharp, arrogant remarks that were made to him by Melanie when he raised questions about the accounts he was dealing with. Mark, a university graduate, was one of those men who looked as if he was going to go far in life. He had worked on a temporary contract at a Merchant Bank and apparently enjoyed the experience. The short sharp replies kept coming and inevitably came the day when Mark had enough, exclaiming that he was not going to continue being spoken to in such a manner and he handed in his notice. Mark headed back to the Merchant Bank and hopefully lived happily ever after.

There are people we meet along the way that are only interested in their own ego and their own self-esteem. Well, Melanie was unfortunately one of those. She, unfortunately, disliked anyone who usurped her, not only regarding her authority but also in the popularity stakes too. I had heard that she was a model in her younger days and brought attention to her husband by being his trophy wife. Well, good for her! But alas her man-management skills were non-existent and she was told so too by Jim, who I will mention later.

When Melanie was in the room, everyone went quiet. All that could be heard was the busy phone calls and the clicking of keyboards. But when the cat was away the mice began to play. We all worked hard, but we allowed ourselves the opportunity to chuckle, to catch up on the office gossip; who was going out with who, discovering each other's interests and what everyone was doing the weekend. Good friendships grew and we were loyal to each other. We comforted each other when the going got tough; the day Julie was in tears because she was not working fast enough on her ledger and she was making mistakes. A rumour spread that Melanie wanted to get rid of Julie. There was no good reason…unless one concludes that it was because Julie had Irish connections. Julie continued to get intimidated and Melanie continued the torture until it made a final head when Julie decided to call a halt to the 'fun' Melanie was having. Julie had worked with NatWest Bank for over 20 years. She had proved her worth with no complaints. So, her argument was, quite rightly, that if she was good enough for NatWest, she was good enough for RB. Melanie backed down, and Julie survived to tell her story. Julie was later to be promoted to team leader. Having words with Melanie certainly paid off in the long run, for her anyway. Others were not so lucky.

Melanie knew how to turn on the charm when she wanted things carried out her way. The champagne flowed when we did her bidding, meeting targets and reducing the debt. We were undeterred because in return we wanted our yearly bonus, something to look forward to at Christmas.

Melanie had her golden boy, the apple of her eye, probably the son she never had. She was to continually confide in him. Mark could do no wrong and if he did, he was soon forgiven. Except on one occasion when the 'BASIL' system was not going smoothly and Mark was reduced to tears. It's hard to see a man cry. I always think when a man cries then the pain must hurt. The team was somewhat amused about the BASIL system the bank had introduced. Firstly, because it was pronounced like the herb by some and BA-SIL by others. Mark remarked, "Whatever, basil or ba-sil, it's useless," and so it was. A failure that was later added to the long list of defeats for RB.

Mark was part of the team and a good singer. For a few brief minutes during the day, he would break into song and that was our entertainment. I heard that he had turned down a recording contract, but I never heard why, that was his secret. I found Mark to be variable, like the weather. One day he was everyone's pal and the next he was having a witch-hunt. Usually, it was Edward. His father was Italian and he had a Belgian grandmother, and an Irish one too! He became the target, defending his case like a wounded soul, claiming that he had done what he had been told to do. Edward had a link with Ireland. Is there a pattern unfolding?

Wayne and Matthew did not last too long after both had words with Melanie and that ended their employment. Matthew went to be a sales representative with a company car, a Volvo, much to the disdain of Melanie. Wayne turned to an online company and we heard he was doing very nicely.

Speaking of Matthew and Wayne, I remember they were late one morning and were promptly given detention. They had to make up the time lost at the end of the day. In I strolled the same day late, just my luck! I got detention too, much to the amusement of my comrades in crime! My reason was that my car had broken down and I had to wait for Green Flag to come and rescue me. Lesley, the team leader, protested my innocence as my situation was not planned. No, Melanie insisted I did the time.

I guess the biggest surprise was the demise of Jim, a gentleman closer in age to Melanie than the rest of the team. Jim had been a manager for British Gas. Because of his experience, he managed the corporate ledger. Jim objected to being treated like an eight-year-old and during a heated meeting behind closed doors, he told Melanie his thoughts. Jim was not imagining things, it was true, and Melanie would ask him a question but would not wait for the reply. She had asked the question and replied to the question herself. Jim told Melanie that she did not have man-management qualities. How true that was. The more her confidence grew the more her arrogance did too. Unfortunately, this is a common trait amongst heads of departments. In their eyes, staff become outlaws of society. Melanie disliked people who could think on their feet. I fell into this category and learnt of this from Lesley, a team leader. Jim was to leave the business, which was a sad day because he was a nice man to work with.

Melanie really should have had robots working for her. She disliked people who outshone her in any way. She wanted to be the belle of the ball. She boasted about her designer shoes, her designer outfits. Her jewellery sparkled and dazzled and the pens she used were rolled gold. No 'Bic' pen for her. *'Good luck to her,'* I thought. It's her money and the shops are there for everyone. No one has a monopoly on shopping. What I do dislike is people who have everything and yet deny other people the same lifestyle.

An insight into her way of thinking happened in 2005. I was speaking with an NHS Director during the course of a day's work. The division had lost one of the accounts to a competitor. But he was pleased now with the service and how the other accounts were being managed that I was providing. He advised me to escalate the advice to submit the tender again. Good news! But Melanie's face was a killer when she was told.

Melanie thought that she was a dab hand at seeing inside people and knowing about their social standing. She said of Edward that he would not be a man to wear an evening suit and bow tie. It was a statement without foundation. Edward was well used to dressing to suit the occasion. He was a rugby player for a local team and also represented Italy in the game. So, for the award dinners, he had to dress to impress.

But that was Melanie, jumping to conclusions. Because I was a single woman, she concluded that I must be a lesbian! Which I hasten to add I am not. Sadly, Alan, my soulmate, died suddenly of a heart attack. I was asked directly by Mark, Melanie's right-hand man, was I a lesbian. Another reference to that 'title' was when I was telling Lesley about going to the theatre to see 'Mrs Brown's Boys'. At the time, it was not on television as it is today. I was explaining to Lesley about Brendan O'Carroll, a popular Irish comedian dressing as a woman and creating a comedy play about a Dublin family. Melanie was passing and heard the conversation and replied, "Oh, I thought you were going to see a woman undressing." I was not impressed and rather disgusted and I said so to Lesley, but knowing Melanie it was best to keep quiet.

Melanie was clever at creating an illusion, not so much by what she said, but rather by what she did not say. 'Hmm' to a statement or 'you' to point directly at someone when wishing to discredit that person. I guess for many who reach the dizzy heights of 'head' of a department, they become untouchable power-wielding warriors, ready to slay another that comes close in mental agility.

Davina, a sociable, nice background sort of girl, who loved her horses and was a hard worker, even came into the line of torment. Melanie told her that she did nothing more than press buttons all day! I bet that it was more than that to Davina. Davina and I were appointed to compile a training manual. We worked together in harmony and had nearly got the job done when Melanie interfered. But there was a method in her madness. By finishing off the task, she was then able to blow her own trumpet and it was 'all hail, Melanie' from senior management.

The perception was a good cover-up in the bank, as long as things looked good on the surface, then all was well. The perception was also an excuse for dismissing individuals too and hiding faults. The perception holds no foundation in law or to trained management teams. Evidence is the real clue to how everything is progressing.

There have been a few books written about the downfall of 'Fred, The Shred', his arrogance, greed, ruthlessness, ambition and recklessness, what happened? Whatever it lead to a downward spiral through the ranks.

For myself, I was the high-flyer, the person who managers went to for assistance in solving account problems, even when the account was not mine to resolve. The praise was done in writing by emails and letters from all levels of management, from colleagues and customers. I believed in giving the best, doing my best and achieving success. Unfortunately, persons with big egos to support do not like competition, and Melanie was one of those individuals, but she was not on her own.

There were quite a few accounts to resolve and tidy up that were not mine to do. I was approached by business account managers arriving at my desk with anxious faces claiming that customers were giving them a hard time, and no doubt they were. An account that springs to mind is the account for British Ports. This customer had several accounts, several direct debits all set up to the wrong port accounts. Holyhead Port billed as Southampton Port and more besides. The mega issues took three days to put right. I assisted the help of two people to do the admin work.

A meeting was then arranged with representatives from British Ports, the business manager, Matt, Diane, who made a ham-fisted attempt at managing the account, and myself. The meeting went well, only marred by Diane's 's attempt to sound important but what came out was a lot of waffle!

But that was one of Diane's characteristics. Her background was Asian. At times, she could be kind and considerate. Given power and the ruthless side of her personality shone out. Her ploy was that she sold people short. She would be the 'snitch', and she made complaints about staff when there were no complaints to be made.

The success of her actions depended on the calibre of management involved. If Diane found an ally, then there was no stopping her. She had an ally in Melanie. Diane's excuse for her actions was 'its office politics'. To deliberately set a plan to destroy a person's excellent reputation to gain her own rise up the ladder is in my opinion the lowest of the low. When a person has to stoop that low in life, then they must be no good in the first place. Rise to fame on your own merits and skills. Believe me, I told her so, in a straight sentence without the urge to be vindictive.

I may have mentioned earlier that Diane told Lesley that the ledger I worked on was not the real deal. What planet was she on! I was managing the NHS/Public Sector accounts throughout the country, Scotland and Wales. Luckily, Lesley was not going to tolerate such bitchiness – with a capital B. We had team leaders that should not have had the responsibility they had been given by senior management. I later discovered it was not because of their brain power. No. The skill was to bully and enjoy doing it!

Diane the centre of bullying activities, when she got the title of team leader, she was on a roll! I remember one sunny afternoon I took a phone call from a customer. My colleague Andrew was handling an issue for this customer. I took the information and duly gave it to Andrew. Then slam, bang, wallop. I was cornered in the 'breakout' area of the office by Andrew, Julie and Diane with the burning question, why had I given the phone message to Andrew? I explained the reason why, while my stomach tied in knots. Not because I was scared of Diane, but I was getting tired of being 'pulled' to one side for a reprimand for no good reason. Diane saw me as a threat to her climb to the top. In time, she was to fall off the ladder and end up working for a cable company.

Before her fall, I was the target of her nastiness a few times, with questions such as: Why did I not have the stereotyped characteristics of the Irish? Why did I not drink? Why did I not have a temper? Along with a string of questions: Why did I not have grey hair like Julie? Why did I not dress like Julie? Weird questions. Julie and I were work colleagues, not joined at the hip because we both had Irish connections.

21

She decided to have a training session for the credit controllers. I was singled out as the one who needed the most training. Diane, the bitch, was not going to give up easily. Fortunately for me, Mark overheard her and in front of the team said, "You will not include Alice. She is an experienced senior credit controller." Her plan was foiled for now, until I was again cornered in the, yes, 'breakout' area of the office. This time, it was the claim I was not working, I was assisting Lesley H., who was to take over the Public Sector ledger from me with how to manage the ledger, deal with issues and how the NHS managed their accounts or used management agents to be more precise. Julie was used as Diane's sidekick, so I had a rant from them both, how the world was not all about me! Where on earth were they coming from? What was the gibberish about? It made no sense, but it was another scheme by Diane to discredit me. The situation was getting out of hand. There was no one I could turn to and Diane knew it. I was coming to the end of my tether with them. How much more could I take from them? When was it going to stop? I was never a person to shout or get into arguments, I was not going to begin now. Julie took me aside and apologised for doubting my integrity and that I had discussed the project with the assistant team manager. I accepted her apology but the tears fell, I could not help myself. It was a thing I had never done in the workplace. At the back of my mind, I thought maybe it will show them that I am human, not so professional I had no feelings.

Irish Eyes Can't Hide Forever

Have you ever done things, gone along with suggestions or ideas to please someone, to keep the peace? It is very difficult when it is your head of the department that makes a request. A request that I think none of the team felt comfortable with. I certainly did not. None of us protested, but somehow it was in everyone's expression, the feeling of that underlying reason why we were being asked to play this game. We all knew Melanie. There was always a pen ready to take notes on what she heard or saw. Even for a musical quiz for 'fun', the pen would be busily scratching away.

This time the rule of the 'game' was to bring in items that highlighted our interests, that told the team something that they did not know about us. The items were: a picture, a poem/prose, a piece of music and an object. Hindsight is a clever thought after an event. This is true in my case. What I should have hidden was my Irish culture, but on the other hand, why should I? I had nothing to be ashamed of, I had done nothing wrong. I only know my Ireland by its music and song, not anything else.

The objects I brought with me were my mum's favourite music on CD. 'The Meeting of The Waters' written by Thomas Moore. It has close links for me too, the place as a holiday destination in beautiful County Wicklow, the garden of Ireland, and the links to my mum's family roots. My red shawl embroidered with a harp and shamrock, which had been part of my Irish dancing costume. I used to do Irish dancing when I was very young. A poem entitled 'The Family', a short piece about the value of being part of a family. And finally, a picture of a two-seater plane, which I thought would be something interesting and different. I was lucky to achieve an ambition of having the experience of sitting in the cockpit of a plane, to feel the excitement of looking down at fields, buildings and objects, and the noticeable feeling of going to fall off the side as land and sky became one. There would have been no way I would have obtained that dream without the flying skills of Anthony, my cousin Mary's husband. Anthony was a flying instructor for an aero club near Dublin airport.

The team meeting came to an end, and generally, there was a sense of relief, however, it was interesting listening and viewing the items that everyone brought in. Throughout the 'meeting' Melanie was as usual busily writing notes. Wish I knew what she was writing down, what morsel of information written down to use in evidence for a later date. It was meant to be a bit of light-heartedness, but there was always a hint of something more serious.

From that day, the atmosphere changed to a coolness. I continued to work as normal, producing the right figures to meet targets. When spoken to, there appeared to be contempt, a snappish tone accompanied instructions. I hoped it would pass. Helen, an experienced senior credit controller, was assigned to work alongside me, managing the Public Sector ledger, which had grown in size. Helen was very easy to work with, although got a bit agitated with Melanie's golden boy who would wind her up throughout the day. It was his amusement. Later, it was Mark who got the blame for Helen losing her job at RB He had the ability to influence Melanie. I do not know the full story, only that it related to a situation on the home front, or so the office grapevine reported. It was a sad day when Helen cleared her desk and packed her bag and walked away. A few years later she was still being missed by colleagues and her name was mentioned often. There are people who give a favourable impression and then leave a void when they leave.

Melanie had strong willpower, but she was influenced by her own jealousies, which clouded her judgement somewhat. Ian was brought in to replace Helen. I was again lucky. He was a hard worker and we worked well as a team. Between us, we tracked down lost vehicles, vehicles that should have been returned to the depot due to end-of-lease contracts and other reasons. Ian used to say that we were like Dempsey and Makepeace, we made such a good team (a popular detective programme at the time).

We all laid low, carried on with our daily work, but the sniping had started and the atmosphere changed. Elaine moved out of Credit Control, declaring that she never wanted to work for Melanie again. Melanie had lost the gloss. The suits became less noticeable, the hair less styled and whatever the reason, we were getting the fallout.

We had our end-of-month team meetings. It was a torture, and no one felt they could be themselves. We reported our monthly targets reached, answered the questions asked, and dearly hoped that nothing more would be queried or analysed. We were asked for ideas, which were taken on board, but Melanie claimed the credit. I hated the ice-breakers. I always felt watched and I watched as notes were taken. The ice-breakers were always silly, suited more to juniors at a primary school than grown adults. So, life plodded on in Credit Control, with the occasional social outing for meals as part of a team-building exercise. I remember we went to Hall Green Dog Stadium, where we hired a private box. It turned out to be an enjoyable evening.

Linda came to work with us on a temporary basis and did not stay for too long. Linda had a pleasant personality, a good sense of humour and fitted in with the team very well. Linda hoped that she would be made a permanent member of staff. She worked hard, met the deadlines. But there appeared to be a coolness between Melanie and Linda. Then the truth was revealed that Linda was told she would not be allowed to stay. When her temporary contract came to an end, so did Linda. Linda talked openly about her love of Ireland and the family holiday that was booked for the summer holidays. Oh, dear! Was that her downfall or just a coincidence?

The CEO left suddenly one morning – a case of here today, gone tomorrow. Rumours spread around the office as usual, but I cannot remember what it was now. The trouble with rumours is you never really know what the truth is or not. It was followed by another scandal about a female director; how she had been side-lined in decision-making. She claimed unfair dismissal and was reported to have lost her case. Again, how did the staff know she lost? It could have been a deterrent to stop anyone else from going down the tribunal route.

The next rumour doing the rounds was that we were to move offices, where and when no one knew. We played the waiting game. It was no good asking questions. It appeared to make senior managers more aloof. We were finally informed that we would be moving to Brindley place in Birmingham. Heck, we were going into the city centre, clinging onto the edge of the rejuvenation area of the city centre. Travelling plans were being made, bus and train timetables were requested, parking concerns were being raised. It was the route to nowhere and the worries seemed to escalate. Management was eager to explain that premises had been sought nearer the current offices in Solihull, but there was no luck there. It was a silly claim really because RB wanted to place its businesses in one area, hence Brindley place.

So began the process of preparing to move offices. By this time, our CEO was Con Baylis, a tall man with fair hair, probably looked younger than his years. He appeared amicable, but not a man who was easy to interpret. There was an 'outing' to our new offices, so we all climbed on board coaches and so began our adventure to the dizzy heights of Brindley place. We could not complain about the building, it was shiny and glossy with large windows from where we could view the Birmingham landscape. The blinds on the windows had to be pulled down to the same level on all floors. This was the job for staff employed by the building management, apparently on the important instructions of Fred Goodwin. The building was to be run on the grading of a hotel. Two restaurants, one serving hot food and the other sandwiches, baguettes, etc. Bins were to be emptied twice a day by staff wearing black trousers and white shirts, finished off with black waistcoats and black ties. These uniforms must have been so uncomfortable to wear for carrying out catering and cleaning tasks, and in the summer months work must have been unbearable. Senior managers considered t introducing uniforms for all staff at RB Vehicle Division. The uniforms were placed on view. They were made of a cheap blue material and would not have made the wearer feel confident. The staff were not opposed to wearing a uniform – it had its advantage in that the women would not have to be fashion-conscious. I am sure envy would have still existed, for the simple reason some women look great in any clothing, designer or not.

In a way, it was a sad day when we left the offices in Solihull. It was an old, tired building, but somehow it was cosy, if you can imagine what I mean. It was familiar. We had the shops to browse around and the local pubs for a quick bite to eat. The main loss was the short trip home at the end of the day. Home was close, within twenty minutes, and our time was our own.

Brindley Place, Here I Come!

In 2006 we headed to Brindley place. I had made an arrangement with two colleagues to car share, at a price, of course, the fuel cost. The two colleagues were Gillian and Barbara, both friendly and easy to get on with and provided chat and laughter, which was a delight when stuck in heavy traffic on the Small Heath Highway. We could easily be there for half an hour or more. One evening one of them, I will not say who to save embarrassment, was wishing badly to go to the ladies. We still had quite a journey to go. However, seeing the Birmingham Canal running alongside the main road only added to her discomfort, which was hilarious entertainment for the other two.

The first evening travelling home was a nightmare. We had left the office at five twenty, had a fifteen-minute-plus walk to the Plaza car park, not a mean feat in three-inch heels. We fell into the car, put on our seat belts and away we went. We got past the Five Ways and then onto Belgrave Road, then there was a traffic diversion due to a bad accident. Great, no sat nav, no map, the diversion signs were of no use to us. Each of us knew bits of the route home. It was definitely not direct, and we went through Kings Heath, on through Shirley, through Hall Green…where were we heading? We were getting tired and hungry, the hands on the in-car clock were ticking away the time. Then suddenly I recognised a road. We were on the home straight, to yelps of delight. It was nearly quarter to eight in the evening when we got home. How we missed our old office in Solihull, despite the glossy, state-of-the-art office we had left over two hours earlier. That was the worst journey home. More often than not we were home by half six.

The first day itself at Brindley place went all right. We were shown to our desks, the computers were set up and the new phones all in matching black. Melanie had placed a small gift bag on each chair, a nice gesture. The bag consisted of a stress ball, to help us get over the dizzy heights of being on the sixth floor, and pieces of stationery to help us with our tasks. It was a strange feeling looking out across the city through floor-to-ceiling glass. Poor Melanie was suffering as she had no head for heights. There were times when we knew Melanie was a human being when she cried almost every day when her sister was diagnosed with cancer. But there were times when she showed another side to her character when she could show disdain for other people's lives. Helen had to have time off to look after her sick child. Melanie berated her saying that she should have got a neighbour to look after her child, which was rather ridiculous – what neighbour would want that responsibility? Melanie was reported to have said, "If you can't look after your child, why to have them in the first place?" Harsh to say the least. If what I was told was true, then that is a double standard in my mind. Basically, do as I say, rather than do as I do.

A Flash to the Past

Relating the latter, it reminds me of an incident in the Civil Service, the department of Social Security. On the management 'throne' was a woman, Miss Bernadette James. She was a difficult person to deal with. She had a reluctance to listen to anyone with a differing opinion. Somehow, most women seem to have a problem with that aspect of management. They are unable to understand, business is business and pleasure is pleasure, it becomes a personal thing. She was arrogant and ruthless, her opinion counted and no one else's. She could not see reason or logic if it bit her on the nose. As is the situation, persons have people on their side, as I did in Paula and Geoff, who held meetings with her to promote me. She would not budge, and the best I achieved was a temporary promotion which lasted three years! When she did retire, there was nobody sad to see her go. Gone was the wicked witch of the west. What a tragic legacy to leave behind, not a proud one that is for sure. Power is a dangerous commodity in the wrong hands! She had her devotees too, such as Mr Hewson, a churchgoer with an attitude. I 'bumped' into him one day out shopping. I had left my employment with the DHSS (Department of Health and Social Security) and he enquired where I was now working. I innocently and politely replied that I was employed by the NEC. His reply was, "How did you get that job?" I was startled and, as is often the case, I got tongue-tied. It was not an answer I was expecting. I realised I should have questioned him on his statement. I never had an argument or disagreement with him, so what was his issue?

There were two sisters, Shirley and Mary. Both were of Irish descent, both struggled to get a promotion. Mary was the first to be demoted, on the pretence that her training had not been successful. Alarm bells rang loudly for the parents when Sheila became the next target. Their father, a strong, determined Irishman, met with Miss J. and that put the clamp on her scheme.

Unfortunately, a senior HEO got injured in the Birmingham Pub Bombings; her hearing was affected in one ear. However, we Irish carried the connection and we paid the price. No matter how young and incapable we were of such an atrocious act, we were all branded the same. In later years, I discovered that Margaret Thatcher was strongly against the Irish, describing us as liars and not to be trusted on any level. For an intelligent woman, it was a very unintelligent statement to declare, but I was to discover that there are two types of intelligence. Firstly, the book-learning intelligence and secondly, the natural intelligence that shines through in people who can 'think on their feet', who have the ability to look at situations rationally.

Sadly, a woman, also named Melanie, still at the Civil Service, would overwrite people's gradings on their job appraisals, giving a lower grading than expected. I had to contend with her as a manager, quietly carrying on with my work, meeting the targets, no arguments, no ifs and buts. But she had the power and she used it.

I was shocked to discover I was her next target. My gradings on my job appraisal had been overwritten and I wanted to know why. A meeting was arranged with her, her senior manager and myself. She, Melanie, was unable to justify what she had carried out, which only highlighted her own shortcomings. Her senior manager, a man who could see through her scheme and who could not contend with the situation any longer, jumped up from his chair, walked to the window and said, "What right have we got to play God with other people's lives?" He handed in his notice soon afterwards and left.

How right he was. A manager's role is to manage staff for the good of the business. It is not a licence to destroy good characters, destroy reputations, mostly carried out based on petty dislikes and prejudices, without a moment's thought for the individual's wellbeing. Being Irish was definitely a dislike and I was constantly criticised about the tone of my voice! My thoughts – if a drama director at the Birmingham Repertory theatre considered I had good dictation and tone, then that was good enough for me.

Yet another woman, Christine, who decided on hearing that most of her team had Irish connections placed a sign on the office door with the words 'Irish foreign office'. None of us liked the gesture but kept quiet as anti-Irish management would be delighted at the first excuse to show us the door.

Senior management ignored these 'goings-on'. They were indifferent. We live in a culture of bullying, and such programmes as 'Big Brother' encourage personalised put-downs. In the House of Commons, included in debates are 'put-downs', but regarded as a bit of fun. No one minds a bit of banter. I refer to the damaging 'put-downs' that cause personal damage whereby there is no return. The person gets into ill-health, loses their job, hence no salary. Character assassination that no one recognises their son's or daughter's description on paper. Remember the proverb, 'sticks and stones may break my bones, but names will never hurt me'? Now the names are harsher and designed to destroy.

As reported in The Irish Post, dated 26th October 2013, an extract of a Gerry Adams interview: "He regrets that the Irish were unsustainable targets of the Troubles," referring to the backlash in Britain. Anti-Irish sentiment already existed here and was simply 'stoked up' by the conflict. People still remember signs in windows by landlords reading 'no dogs, no blacks, no Irish'. This was the twentieth century. Surely, intelligent people would be able to judge individuals for themselves on meeting. Apparently not. I was judged by my culture, my connection to another country that I knew very little about. The majority of the Irish people were against the conflict. A great many Irish people served Britain extremely well during the First World War, a fact that was only acknowledged officially last year (2014). During the Second World War, it was an Irishman that shot down more German planes for Britain than anyone else. (Ryan Tubridy's book 'The Irish Are Coming'.)

In the 1970s, the anti-Irish feeling was rife. Yes, understandable to a point. Why suddenly turn on a neighbour who has helped you for years, repairing your roof, painting your walls and building your fences all for free, knowing full well that when bombs were going off in Birmingham city centre your good, helpful neighbour was sitting watching television with the family, equally shocked, stunned and horrified watching the news programme that fateful night. It is impossible to put everyone of a nationality into the same pigeonhole. Judge individuals as individuals.

The Irish are branded as a nation of drinkers, drunk at every opportunity, be it a wedding or a funeral. When the reply to an offer of a drink is 'no thank you, I would rather have a coffee', the astounded expression on the recipient of 'all the Irish drink' is a picture to behold. Don't be so stupid! We are not all drinkers, falling around the pavement at the closing time singing 'The Wild Rover'. We are all individuals, different ideas, opinions, different religious and political views. Guess what? Just like the British people.

At the local 1 Council, out of the blue, I witnessed a conversation between two people. I was working alongside both of them on the same team. The two people were Lisa and Robert, who was far from being a popular member of the staff. He used to irritate senior managers, but it did him no harm. He crept up the promotional ladder with no problem. Back to the conversation between the two. Lisa was saying how the Irish were being treated very badly and that her sister had been a victim of this hatred in the workplace. This was the clue, the secret was out, and anti-Irish feelings were rife.

Robert spent time 'nit-picking' about my work, so I would have to spend time explaining how to do calculations etc. to him. Of course, he was learning. I asked to speak with the, Head of Department, about the situation, to no avail, but I learnt later that Robert was her 'golden boy', he could do no wrong, she would go to hell and back for him. Her response to me, "I knew this was going to happen." How did she know? And if so, why did she not do something about Robert's attitude? I was later to hear her referred to as 'Teflon Jan'.

I believe I had a good manager in Diane, who acknowledged the fact that on arriving at the Council I had played a major role in organising the new billing system, which I had made my own success.

I applied for team leader positions, but what a waste of time, there was no chance. A performing monkey would get the promotion before me. I trained other staff. Staff would come to me for advice on how to do a task, and I was in demand. I was popular within the office and other departments, I met my work targets, what more did they want?

Harry, the previous Head of Department, told me when questioned, "I was overlooked." It is astonishing what comes out of the mouths of some of these managers. I was advised that I do the supervisory work of someone who had got promoted as I knew how to do it and she did not! I needed the patience of a saint. I stated my views but never lost my temper with them. I was never a hothead, so I was not going to start now.

Derek, my immediate manager, got the push out the door. A well-managed plan by Robert and Harry who apparently, if the rumour is true, wanted to be rid of Derek 1 from the start. Derek admitted to me that I should have got promoted. Again, I got tongue-tied and I was shocked. These managers are responsible for people's well-being, their lives even. Many staff are treated by power-crazed, arrogant individuals, as basically life's shit, with no genuine man-management skills. Staff are like throwaway paper cups, with at times a total disregard for their staff. I am well aware that many of these so-called managers are there because of their right circle of friends in the workplace.

Please do not misjudge that I am anti-management or anti-establishment. I am certainly not. I trained as a retail manager and currently, I am a career coach, running my own business. I strongly believe that a manager has a duty of care to speak with staff, and understand the importance that managers have in people's lives. Integrity is a vital ingredient. Why insult a member of staff for no reason, make accusations that are untrue, or destroy people's good character…Why? For fun? For kicks? Using staff as 'punch bags' on a bad hair day to satisfy over-inflated egos. Wake up! You're not Gods! But you think you are. I was told I had skeletons in the cupboard! I was told I had baggage! Where did all that nonsense come from? Well, you got it wrong. I have neither. I come from a well-respected Catholic family with no skeletons in any cupboard unless you call being Irish a skeleton.

Sadly, Harry's 's daughter got killed stepping out of a taxi. I felt sorry for him, the pain he and his family must have been going through. But I also thought I was someone's daughter. I had a mother and father. I was part of a family, but I did not matter to corporate managers. My feelings did not matter, the feelings of my parents did not matter. I was working hard, probably too hard to prove my talents, the daily statistics proved the point. But for Harry, Janis and Derek, all they saw was the word 'Irish', let's destroy.

I even went ahead and obtained an NVQ in office administration. I wanted then to attain the next level. Guess what? I was advised by my tutor that I would not get the support from management and would therefore struggle to obtain the knowledge to complete the course.

I handed in my notice and wrote a letter to the Personnel department, who duly replied to my letter that they were going to investigate my claim, which they did and the training officer was dismissed, a woman who claimed to like the Irish, but behind the exterior, she had different thoughts. "Come into my office and we can talk if things get too much for you," she would say. "I love the Irish."

Part of me wishes I had continued working at the Council. Would my situation have been changed? Would I have gotten the recognition I definitely deserved? Who knows. On my last day, Janis told me that she was sorry to see me go and if I wanted to go back my desk would be there. I have been told that I was missed by staff, that work was not getting cleared, deadlines were not being met. Basically, how did I manage to meet the targets when I was there! I worked very hard and they knew that. Do they have guilty consciences now? I will never know. But I know one thing for certain – I would not have ended up working for RB, one of the worst employers anyone could work for. They have a disdain for their employees at all levels. The problem with many, not all, managers is that they do not like to be 'bested', black is white if it suits them. The CEO held an 'open floor' meeting for all staff to give ideas on how the business could be improved. I suggested that all staff received quality training – it was very much a mishmash. His grunted response was, "We can't train everyone." Why? How are people to learn the correct processes and procedures? If the training has a good foundation, then all staff will be trained to the same high standard. A sample that immediately comes to mind is that on arriving at the company, I noticed that agreements were not signed by clients, figures altered in pencil and other errors. There was the story that a group of farmers had leased vehicles but not signed paperwork. I can leave it to your imagination what the outcome was…and they say training is not important!

What lengths do employers go to check out the potential of staff? A question I often ask. Are the needs of the business really thought out, taking into consideration the calibre of staff being employed?

Forward to the Present

A long came the arrival of Perry, assistant to Melanie, who generally appeared to be amicable with everyone, laughing, joking and generally listening to the cold facts of Credit Control. Soon he began to struggle with the position, and coming with the struggle and frustration was an opening, revealing a different side to his character.

He was reckless with his tongue. He openly declared that he thought nothing of getting rid of people he did not like. I had no issues with him, but I became a target. He resorted to throwing paperwork at me rather than passing paperwork in a professional manner. I was unhappy, so I let my feelings be known to Lesley. Perry made use of his authority and progressed to complain that I was not entering notes on people's accounts. I was constantly printing out customers' notes to prove that I had made sufficient notes, highlighting dates and times. It was tedious having to do such a task. At the time, maybe I should have had words with him. But there was a turnaround: Perry l had enough and handed in his resignation to Melanie. The turnaround also brought a change in him. He stopped throwing paperwork at me, stopped finding fault with my work. He began giving credit when it was due. I had my job appraisal with him and I was stunned that he advised me to sell myself, not to hide the skills and knowledge that I had and let no one hold me back.

Why did he change from nice to Mr Nasty and back to Mr Nice Guy? Was he instructed to be obstructive? Why was Melanie aware of the situation when I had not made a complaint? Melanie knew how to play people. Setting people against people is a well-known leadership trait but given the upmarket wording of 'influencing' people.

Perry's name was to be mentioned again. It was before he had left, but it came as a surprise to me and showed me also the danger of surmising a situation or indeed about people. It was a usual working morning, the team managers had disappeared to a meeting. I received a phone call from my mother saying that she felt very unwell. I of course was immediately concerned and reassured Mum that I was coming home. I quickly contacted the doctor for a call-out and phoned for a taxi. Then I had to get permission to go home. Lesley was at the meeting, Mark was there so I asked him. He said ask Melanie. I went to Melanie, who wanted to know had I asked Lesley. Unable to, so I was told to ask Mark. My heart was pounding. I was anxious to get away. What the hell were they playing at? It was not a game to be played out and this was a serious situation. Some staff said I should have just gone, but that would have given Melanie the opportunity to 'have a go' at me. Unfortunately, there are people in this life who delight in watching and waiting for faults to be committed so they can go on a torrent of anger against the person.

Mark said yes, so I raced off. Luckily, by the time I had reached the ground floor from the sixth floor, the taxi was waiting for me. An eight-mile journey filled with anxiety. The journey felt longer. I was wishing the taxi to go faster, the traffic lights to be on the green. Then I arrived at home to the release of stress for my pale, tired and definitely-something-wrong mum. I was at home to take care of everything, to make everything better if I could. The doctor arrived soon after me. Mum's new prescription was the problem and this was quickly altered. I stayed at home for two days with Mum to ensure that she was well and back on track. Of course, I informed Lesley of the situation each day, as per the rules and regulations.

On my return to work, Melanie informed me that the two days would be classed as holiday leave. I accepted the decision. There was no why, if, buts or maybe, because the most important thing to me was that my mum recovered. The days passed and I thought no more. At the time, I was sorting out a future pension matter with the HR department. Lesley was aware of the matter, both as my team leader and a friend. HR were taking longer to resolve the paperwork than was usual and failed to keep to the deadlines stated in their correspondence to me. So, I had to make a few phone calls to HR. *'No problem in that respect, or so,'* I thought. While on the phone I enquired as to what constituted emergency leave and if annual leave could be deducted. You, the reader, can guess the answer. That's right, annual leave was not to be deducted in emergencies. I informed Lesley as a friend, who asked Perry. He agreed with the answer and advised Lesley to speak with Melanie.

Wow, what a reaction from Melanie! She grabbed her pen and her large notebook, turning the page to a clean one as she walked, demanding to me that she wanted a word. Oh heck. Melanie was on the war path. Why? What was she afraid of? After all, it was my pension I was dealing with, it was my annual leave I was enquiring about. We were in an open-plan office, so eyes were upon us. The maintenance team were eyeing each other. What had taken place? What had I done to make Melanie so tetchy and go red in the face?

Melanie, Lesley and myself sat at a round table to the side of our section, Melanie with her gold pen poised to write down all the details. What she hoped to hear I don't know. I explained the reason why I was phoning HR and the question about annual leave. Melanie ranted away that because I did not phone before 8.30 A.M. to inform them that I would not be at work, this was being held against me. I went on to explain that it was not me that was ill but my mother, therefore I would have to wait and review each day. I was accused of being away because of the treatment I was getting from Perry, the assistant manager. Melanie had made her incorrect assumptions about the situation. It would have to be a person with no principles to make up a story about a member of the family being ill. I was forced into providing my mother's prescription for her to view as proof. I was asked if I had contacted the doctor. I guess people who do underhand things believe that everyone else is doing underhand things too.

Lesley was disgusted and surprised that I did not walk out. Eyes were on us and the jungle drums were in full swing! But I hung on and lived to tell the tale. Many of the staff said that I should have said that my mother was first and foremost and that is the fact, so there! I was told I was too nice and polite with Melanie and should stand up to her. The way to stand up to her would be to get verbally rough with her, but that was not my character or personality.

I was naïve, maybe, but I always believed that if a person was a manager, then they had a duty to do things right regarding the business and the people who worked for them. I continue to believe that as a strong principle. Directors, managers, and team leaders consist of a variety of people, with varying backgrounds, varying morals and principles. Some are 'dragged up instead of brought up', and unfortunately a large percentage fall into that category. When the shoe is on the other foot, how their opinions and attitudes change. It becomes about them; their wife, their sister, their daughter/son…In essence, their feelings and to hell with other people's families. They will willingly pull the rug from under someone's daughter, but no one dares do the same to their daughter.

Viewing Google for tribunal cases taken against the bank, the list is substantial. Some of the cases are somewhat distressing, but the horror is management's indifference to resolve issues internally.

The king of his empire, he believed that he was above everyone…His ego was larger than him. We got an insight into him when he visited the office. He was surrounded by bodyguards, who even stood outside the open doors of the lift he was to use. Waste paper bins were checked for suspicious items before his arrival. We were instructed to remove any paperwork from our desks, the switchboard was turned off while he glanced around the office with his hands in his pockets. What planet was he on? Surely a CEO wants to see business in progress! Surely, the sound of a thriving environment is paramount. Silence was the order of the day.

RB have an online mentoring service for employees. I wonder how many people take advantage of the service. What do they advise regarding the welfare of staff? I doubt if it would be straight or honest. Considering team managers' lack of knowledge on government legislation, such as The Equality Act 2010, which includes discrimination by perception, RB made the decision that they were exempt from such notions, they were above employment law.

7th April 2006
Email Sent to the Team

I went to work following a day's leave, not expecting any dramatics to have taken place in my absence. What was done was underhand and devious and without honesty. Martin, who'd done the dirty deed, was treated to promotion. I suspect that management never found out who the culprit was or maybe they were not that bothered, who knows.

Apparently, a phone call had been made to HR to complain about Melanie's style of management. Thankfully, I was not around at the time. We were all called into a meeting on Monday with Melanie, plus the acting CEO, and the, Head of Department. This followed with 1-2-1 discussions with them too. An email dated 7th April 2006 was quite lengthy, however, here the problem lies and should have been clarified at the time. "There was evidence at least one person had sent more than one written submission. Whilst it was not important to identify each written response, we were able to discuss matters freely with staff."

What were the written submissions? Indeed, did Martin admit what he had done, or was the blame placed on someone else? That is something I will never know.

Message Sent

Dear All

Thank you for your attendance at the team meeting on Monday and your subsequent 1-2-1 discussions with me

I stated at the start of our team session that I take all cases of staff dissatisfaction seriously and it is, for this reason, I invested a lot of my time in personally speaking to you all to address the issues raised. From this, it was my aim to identify how commonplace these issues were and whether or not further action needed to be taken.

The general findings are as follows.

- The overwhelming majority of staff thought that the department was well-run by Melanie, but that the department was suffering undue pressure from matters such as Portfolio to Alfa migration, heavy increase in inbound call traffic and ineffective inter-departmental working.
- More people were willing to support the management of the department and were happy with it. 18 staff spoke very positively about Melanie and were more concerned about equity with other departments and general pressures, not with Melanie's style of management.
- There was evidence that at least one person had sent more than one written submission to me and therefore the number of individual comments was less than twelve. Whilst it was not important to identify each written response, we were able to discuss matters freely with staff who identified their written remarks freely and clarified key points.

The common themes were as follows:

1) The implementation of the group policy on sickness and absence was, in some cases, considered unfair and inconsistent compared to other departments. A further review by me confirms that Melanie fairly and accurately applied the current company view on the policy for sickness and absence management and has no case to answer. I have asked Melanie to circulate the company's rules on this for your attention. My concern is that other departments appear not to be managing this as effectively and this will change moving forward.

2) Holiday management is also effectively managed, but there appears to be a need for flexibility where possible. Melanie believes that she is flexible in this regard but quite rightly has to make sure that holiday booking is planned well in advance. It is sometimes not possible to sanction a day's holiday the day before it is due for operational reasons.

3) *All staff are working under pressure and sometimes delivery style can change. I have asked Melanie to reflect on this and she has been very professional and agreed to do so. The Bank has a Code of Conduct and whilst there was no direct evidence that this was breached, all staff should be aware of the expectations here.*

4) *I identified that two members of the team appeared to have personal problems with Melanie's style and I have asked Melanie to meet with all staff to discuss the matters.*

5) *I have also suggested, following a couple of suggestions from the team, that you need a bit of fun and perhaps a bit of a team build. When Melanie returns from holiday, she will arrange this to release some of the frustrations!*

6) *Some of you thought that Melanie took too much on herself and should let her people manage more and I have suggested to Melanie she takes this on board. For your benefit and hers!*

All in all, your team needs to learn the lessons on all sides, discuss problems with each other more openly and freely and move forward afresh. I know talking to all of you that it is your intention to do.

A Management Character Trait –
Have No Scruples

No scruples existed. The main duty of a team leader was to manipulate, twist the truth, replace good with bad reports. I remember a newly recruited team manager so shocked and stunned by what she heard about the staff at a management meeting that it resulted in her resigning from the business. Unfortunately, she never related what she saw or heard, we can only imagine it must have been unbelievable. The reference she made to the meeting was that 'it made the hairs stand up on the back of her neck'. A good turn done towards a colleague was frowned upon, but where was the harm in doing so? I don't know and I guess I will never know. I was working busily when I noticed that a colleague was missing from her desk for quite a while. Earlier, Lyndsey was complaining of not feeling well; she was having trouble breathing due to asthma. I instinctively went to the ladies' cloakroom to see if she was all right. She was pleased to see me. Lyndsey was struggling to breathe. I did not hesitate to tell Lesley, the team leader, what was happening.

I could see the apprehension in her face, the fear that she had to approach the manager to relate the story…what would Melanie's reaction be? Annoyance? Concern? Well, maybe you have already guessed the response uncomfortable… Lyndsey was allowed to go to the doctor's and Melanie had to tolerate the doctor's annoyance that Lyndsey was sent home alone. However, it did not pay me to do the good deed, if you get my drift. Lyndsey was to stab me in the back, even though in the months to follow I gave her lunch money because she was making 'poor mouth' about her finances. She came to my home to purchase a computer I was selling. She was given a welcome and the usual cup of tea and Irish brack. She complained to the team leader that I was not working because I had left my desk. In her eagerness to bad-mouth me, she did not notice that I was right behind her, photocopying an agreement that a customer had requested.

Needless to say, I never trusted her after that incident, although I still had to work with her and be civil in my dealings with her. Lyndsey knew how to play the corporate game. She landed the prize of the opportunity to go to Celtic Manor, a five-star luxury hotel and golf course in Wales, for an Award Ceremony. She was also awarded £50 for her work on the ledger. They say the devil looks after his own! However, it was my hard work and success prior to her taking over management of the Public Sector ledger that won her the place. A fact that did not go unnoticed by team managers. The last I heard of Lyndsey she went to live down south.

I had an excellent rapport with the business development managers who dealt with the corporate clients. Tom was a BDM, tall, blonde, white South African who would contact me to deal with client issues, although at times the clients were not on my ledger of accounts.

The afternoon was busy, the emails were coming in fast. I noticed an email in my inbox addressed to Melanie. I saw that it was from Tom but I did not read the content because it was not for my attention. With hindsight, I wish I had read it so I could have been on my guard. I was questioned as to why Tom had sent the email to me. I honestly did not know. Melanie asked Sarah, the deputy manager, to phone Tom and explain to him that he was no longer to speak to me about queries. Sarah continued to say, "No, Alice does not mind, but she has her own work to do." Tom never spoke to me thereafter. I wish I had known what was in the email. Whatever happened, the excellent working relationship had been broken, but I guess that was Melanie's motive.

Lyndsey, the backstabbing friend, raised her head again. Sarah, the deputy manager's phone number had been given to a customer and she was irate about it. Lyndsey was eager to tell her that it was me who had given the number to the customer. I denied it because I had not done it. Mark, the team manager, felt sorry for me and investigated the incident. And it transpired that Sarah's phone number had been given to the customer by Blackshoe s Solicitors, the company used by the business. Mark said it was a pity that people did not obtain the evidence before making accusations.

RB worked on the policy that the positives a person had, they would turn the positives into negative character/personality traits. And quite openly use whatever they could to destroy a person. One has to view the internet to see how many tribunal cases were brought against RB. Taking RB to a tribunal was useless. They had top-notch lawyers to 'make mincemeat' of staff, words of the Union representative.

We worked in an environment that at times was unreal. How could people be the way they were with people? What was to be achieved? Nothing. Precisely that. Nothing. The business closed down after the financial crash so nothing was left, only hatred for the banking industry and dislike and bad memories amongst the staff.

It was very easy for staff to 'gang up' on other members of staff. Team managers enjoyed the plots too and some instigated the jealous allegations made against a member of staff. Friends could easily turn against friends, all to gain power and the promise of rewards.

There always seemed to be a variety of ideas floating around, new ideas set up and then forgotten about. There was always a reluctance to admit defeat or admit that something had gone wrong.

Some days, life in the workplace was all right. Thankfully there are good people too. I continued to work hard, bringing in the debt and continually received emails and letters from customers thanking me for my help in resolving issues. There was a rumour going around that a restructure of the people gradings was to take place. The rumour was true. Like nearly everything that the Vehicle Division did was done mostly with no thought to legislation, rules or policies. Every member of staff came face to face with their team managers. My turn came soon enough. I had been a Grade 4, but under the new structure, I would be classed as a Grade 3! Which meant in reality that I would not receive the Christmas bonus. To be eligible for the bonus staff had to be Grade 4 or above. You can imagine the atmosphere and anger amongst the staff. What could we do?

What a mixture of emotions and situations floated throughout the office. It became more and more apparent business was not about managing the business. The business coped because there were people who did care and wanted the business to be the best it could. To many, though, business was about bullying, intimidating staff and reprimanding staff to feed their own egos. And in doing so, never became aware of their own stupidity.

On the 6th September 2006, I received an email from the Assistant Credit Control Manager.

I would ask that this is put into Alice's file and can be used in her one-to-one appraisal. I would like to draw your attention to the very professional manner Alice portrayed with taking ownership for the actions in the Climate Scan update. She has proved to be very detrimental in getting the action started and getting the in-depth information needed to proceed with the team's action plan. Her actions should help to improve the relationships between other departments and free up more time to collect debt and hit the ledgers.

Sounds good. Reads good too, and the email attachment was duly placed in my Personal Development folder. The Personal Development folders were about as much good as a wet weekend when you want to cut the grass. More about those folders in a minute. It is so easy to get side-tracked.

Oh dear, back to the school playground mentality again. Sarah returned after a day's leave and I was ushered to the breakout area. I was beginning to dread that area of the office and who could blame me. I was ushered to the said area and I followed like an obedient child, bracing myself at the same time for some silly accusation…and how right I was. I was being reprimanded by Sarah for sitting at her desk when she was on leave. Melanie had told her. For heaven's sake! Was this conversation really taking place in a business that was a division of an international corporate empire? As always, I remained calm and explained that there was a shortage of seating and Mark told me to sit at her desk. I definitely left her desk as I had found it – tidy. I had not done anything inappropriate, but that is how the business was managed. I did confide in Mark about how I felt about the current situation. Needless to say, he was not happy either. He knew things were getting out of hand. How long was the situation to last? What was their game? Mark said that I had more knowledge and experience than Sarah and Diane . He said that he would ask Sarah if I could assist Diane with team leader duties and train new staff. This course of action was written on my Personal Development Plan.

These Personal Development Plan folders were jammed-packed with information on courses taken within the office and online courses. The online courses were designed and produced by Harvard Business School, with assessment tests giving a score. I was fortunate. I always got high scores. It was interesting how someone in the business can spot details about an individual, an individual that does not work with them. This happened to me. I had to phone the department that dealt with the online assessment tests, as I was unable to

45

access the test for that month. When I said my name, his reply both surprised and delighted me. "I recognise your name, you always get a high score on the tests, you're consistent."

At a team meeting, Sarah said, "A couple of people stood out on the section and she was going to put a stop to that." Diane had an ally. She was eager to get to the top and use whatever tactics she could. Such a statement is a licence to destroy other people, and believe me, there are those people who are only too willing to act upon those words.

Diane took advantage of the offer. When cornered about her actions, her reply was always 'it's office politics'. I remember telling her that it was more rewarding getting a promotion on one's own merits, rather than on the back of another person, or indeed destroying someone else to get there. At the time, I was not happy that she put on my job appraisal that I went to Credit Control with a query about an excess mileage invoice. It was a ridiculous thing to write. I was a senior credit controller. I think that tells it all.

The comments go on and on, always with audience: "You are dealing with complex queries now, which is good."

"You don't like being on the phone."

It got worse. It was getting to breaking point. I could no longer give ideas or ask questions. I was either ignored or received a gruff, impertinent reply. The personal comments increased to make me feel uncomfortable. "Why did I not have grey hair?" "When was I going to retire?" "At my time of life, I should not be thinking of getting on in the business." Melanie put her penny's worth in too: "At our age, we have to think of our pensions." I know nowadays pensions are a consideration at an earlier age, but comments like that in the workplace come under the heading of age discrimination.

Of course, there were the good days, happy moments with colleagues from other areas of the business. Previous to the bad stuff I came forward with suggestions, as Stuart requested for staff to do. On the 9th May 2007, I sent an email to the acting CEO:

This is just a suggestion: Would it be a good idea if the encoders had a checklist of actions taken on each agreement that was encoded? It would act as a double-check on the information being input on the system. The encoder would tick and sign the boxes to confirm the action take...e.g. name and address checked, vehicle registration checked, vehicle make and model checked, direct

debit passed to Activation, cheque received and passed to Finance. Finally, the
form could be kept in the agreement file for reference.

Regards,
Alice

I got a reply back from, approximately forty minutes later:

Great idea. I will ask Niki and Romanda to pick this up as part of the stability
piece.
Many thanks.

I continued to work hard on the account ledger, the PF ledger as it was known because the accounts began with those letters. These were Broker accounts, whereby customers took out the agreement via a firm of brokers. I moved on from these accounts to Recovery accounts, dealing with customers that had failed to pay. I was able to have a rapport with customers. I always believed it was wise to set up an instalment plan rather than be so eager to take some to court. It is only fair. They say a little knowledge is a dangerous thing, but having too much knowledge can be just as bad. Yes, I had a lot of knowledge, and because of that, I ended up working on all the ledgers when someone was away sick, on leave or if they were struggling to manage the accounts and not attaining the debt reduction figures. I did not object, I obeyed the orders as instructed.

I continued to receive 'thank you' emails and letters, internally and externally. I kept them all in my PDP folder. The comments were a delight to receive, it showed I was very good at what I did.

The Root of All Evil

It has been said many times that money is the root of all evil. Maybe so, but I believe that jealousy is the root of all evil. Jealousy knows no bounds. It becomes a 'bug' within the person, eating away at their self-respect and common sense. And more often than not, making them look stupid amongst colleagues.

But these individuals throw caution to the wind. They take chances and hope vigorously to come out on top. Many succeed, others are not quite so lucky. It mostly depends on where the individual comes in the pecking order.

Pecking being the operative word. There, lurking in the background, was the eager tendency to look for faults in people, nit-picking at its best. The amount of energy spent in this activity was better than a marathon. If half the energy was used in positive concerns for the business, then the business need not have died. The Division could have survived the closure imposed by RB, who were restructuring divisions and closing others. I guess that is another story. When people don't see the wood for the trees or are so caught up in their individual agendas, they don't see anything.

Did I work too hard for my own good? With hindsight, the answer is yes. I was too clever, too observant and considered other colleagues. They got respect and thoughtfulness too. Probably sounds as if I am shining my own halo! But facts are facts regardless of who is doing the talking.

People forget what they have said, what orders they have given or what instructions they handed out. That's fine, that is life, and as long as no one gets hurt in the process and matters can be rectified that's all right. It's when a person forgets and then keeps a mental note of 'it's another person's fault' and then even after events have been explained to them, still continue to blame the other person! That is the ruthless outcome of a jealous person.

I was working with Iain. We were a good team, resolving issues and tracing vehicles. We were ace. Things were tense on another team working on the 'core' ledger. The debt was not coming in as fast as it should have been. So Iain and myself were called to the rescue, meaning of course we fell behind with our work. Melanie came swiftly to us one day, asking what was going on, that our work had fallen short. Had she forgotten what she had said? Who knows, but there was no doubt in her eagerness to pounce on us to provide an explanation. If, on the other hand, she had forgotten, her approach would have been calmer and more considered.

Please don't get me wrong, if I had done something wrong, then quite rightly I would take ownership. I will admit that I did not like being blamed for something that I played no part in. There were times I believe they wanted me to take the blame regardless. I remember being reprimanded about something that did not involve me and told to just take the reprimand and forget about it. Sorry, no can do. It's not in my personality and I would not expect anyone else to take the blame, if they were innocent.

However, the business world continued, blame or no blame. I continued to receive acknowledgement from various departments and customers. But there lurking was the displeasure of any praise that came my way. It was my turn to work the late shift, as we called it. It was about five o'clock when, a Business Development Manager came to me. Matt was one of those men who stood out from the crowd, a tall dark-haired man with chiselled looks and very good taste in his appearance. He was in good spirits and told his story of how the BDMs had gone for a curry with the 'acting' CEO. Matt was discussing a particular difficult account with him whereby the customer wanted to cancel the contracts. Matt explained to him about the work I had carried out to rectify the situation and the customer retracted their request to cancel agreements. Matt was delighted and wanted to tell me the good news that the CEO had recognised my ability in rescuing the situation. He was going to tell the good news to Melanie the next day. Which he duly did. But no, Melanie was not going, to be honest, in the praise. She sent an email to the whole team congratulating everyone on the praise received from the sales team. What could I do? I was faced with a losing battle. Yes, I wanted to get on in the business, I wanted to achieve real recognition. And why not? I was told at my age why did I want to achieve success, should I not want to take life easy! What age did they think I was? I was years away from retirement and not something I was contemplating soon. Nothing made any difference.

Inside my body, I was upset. My instinct was to remain professional at all times. I only allowed the tears to fall when I went to the ladies cloakroom, no one could see me there. There were times five o'clock could not come soon enough for me. I had followers within the office, unfortunately not colleagues with power and authority to help me. It was a weird environment to work in. I had never experienced anything so lacking in professionalism and underhand dealings with each other. At times, I wondered if these people were human. They were like cavemen and women, scavenging for 'dropping' people in trouble. I was even advised to come into work, get on with the job, say nothing, hear nothing and go home at the end of the day, don't even try to fix anything, be invisible. That was a difficult task. I was not a robot, I had talent and I wanted to use it. I strongly believed the business would have benefited in some small way, or maybe even bigger.

I discovered along the way that some vehicles were standing on dealer forecourts not being collected. Surely, the revenue would have added up substantially to make it a worthwhile task to bring in those vehicles. Maybe not. My suggestion was met with coldness and disinterest or was that just to me and behind closed doors the business was grateful. I so wanted to be alive, enthusiastic as always and never give up. I was always creative and took my opportunity. Sarah decided that instead of submitting our ledger figures in the usual format at the team meeting, we should present them in a different way. Julie presented her report on PowerPoint. Different, but not interesting. I presented mine in a totally different way, by issuing them as front top stories in a newspaper, aptly named 'Sundry Debtor News'. It was fun, and everyone seemed to enjoy it, some more than others. Julie won the prize, but I got the more expensive chocolates. There were of course snippets of merriment, like 'Spin the Wheel', and I won a prize for good customer service, along with 'You're A Star'. I was even offered a spa day at Hoar Park. I declined the generous offer for personal reasons, not because I was being obstinate. Lesley said that if I were a man, I would be sitting alongside the directors working. I knew my stuff. Maybe there is an element of truth in the statement. We had already seen the demise of the one and only woman director in the business. As I write this paragraph, I remember a temporary woman director arrived named Linda. She appeared fair-minded, with the ability to listen to staff, although for a vague and strange reason I was brought into her office to be blamed for something I had no knowledge about. I felt rather uncomfortable about the situation. She listened and, in a way, looked just as bewildered as I must have looked too. Unfortunately, her position was only temporary and she was gone, out of a man's world. Before she left, I got an email from her dated the 26th March 2010 regarding 'The Fulfilment Monthly' newsletter, of which I was the editor. The email read:

Well done, Alice – to you and the rest of the guys involved in pulling this together. A bit of fun during the day always helps.

It sure does.

I was fortunate to have a good team with me and we enjoyed thinking of new competitions and the prizes to be won. The newsletter faltered after a year, due to that ugliest of traits – jealousy – by a woman who failed to disguise the fact. She deliberately set out to close the newsletter down and succeeded and nobody was fooled into thinking differently.

There are always hidden agendas, a blame culture that allows no peace and it continues when senior management join in. They have a choice to change it but refuse. More often than not it suits their mentality and probably their abilities as managers. They hide behind others and cling to their stablemates for support.

The office parties were not something to be enjoyed, very rarely in fact. Staff only affairs with a strong air of tension, most women vying for attention and getting green-eyed if any other woman outshone and took the limelight. The parties changed over the years, the younger ones took over, forgetting their common sense and forgetting that they stood a chance of becoming a topic of office gossip the next day…on the promotion ladder, they stood to gain! A far from image that a company wanted to be portrayed several years earlier. One party did stand out from the rest, when I danced the evening away with one of the business development managers and enjoyed the food and chat with my co-workers, mingled with compliments from my team manager that I was lovely inside and out. Although the evening began with a slight hiccup when Diane omitted my name on the guest list. I felt hurt at first, not seeing my name on the seating plan. Part of me wanted to go home, part of me did not want to be bested into running away.

I knew I was not the only member of staff to suffer. Joan had spent the day happily working away and when she was having her tea that evening, she received a phone call to advise her that she was no longer required and she was to leave at the end of the month.

No one dared challenge a team leader. Whatever the situation was, how ethical the manager was being, it was best to go with the flow. Sitting on my ledger was seventy thousand pounds credit, there because various accounts departments within a Public Sector organisation were incompetent of managing the accounts. There it was until a manager decided to help another internal department with a shortfall on their accounts, or so I was told at the time. Overnight it disappeared, but that figure was to come to the surface a couple of times during my stay at the office. Firstly, when we were told by a CEO that we were to 'fill our boots' and apply to go on training courses etc. because there was a sum of seventy thousand pounds in the training fund. When I enquired about a training course, my application got rejected on the grounds that the funding had already been allocated to other projects within the training department.

"Bitches" are to be found everywhere, people who appear all right on the surface, but are your worst enemy, spying and watching for every opportunity to pounce, even for the silliest of reasons. Even the sun shining was a cause for complaint. I was getting to the end of being able to contend with the continuous 'sniping' and 'bitchiness'. Although I made no comment, there was a chance it was in my expression. So much so that Sarah, my team manager, said, "You have had enough, haven't you?" Indeed, I had. She left her desk and returned within a short time and told me to follow her. We went into one of the glass-walled offices and I was met with a surprise. Sitting at the desk was Bill, a team manager from the Metal Support Team, so called because they dealt with complaints about vehicles leased to customers. I did not know what was going to be said to me, but somehow, I felt lighter. It was not going to be bad. I was offered a secondment to his team and that I could go at the end of the week. Hooray! I was out. I could leave the sniping behind. The bitches could get on with their own miserable lives, I was out.

The weekend came and went quickly. They say time goes quickly when you are enjoying whatever you're doing. How true. Monday came quickly. I was free. The Metal Support Team were a good team to work with. We got on with the tasks in hand, and the training given was good. I enjoyed what I did. I was learning more about the business. My happiness was short-lived. Melanie returned from holiday and was far from happy when I was no longer working on her section. She had previously denied me the opportunity to go on a three-month secondment, although she had been offered a temporary member of staff to cover for me. Her 'golden boy' Mark acted as the go-between with me to discuss my return to the section, much to his dissatisfaction. I often wonder why she did not come to me directly. Was she afraid of the truth? Was she made a scapegoat by other people too, people who had their own points to score?

My secondment position was to be made permanent. I completed the job application and obtained an interview. By now, Bill had been transferred to another team. Sandra took his place. She was a fair-minded person with no hang-ups. Everyone was treated the same. The day of the interview came. I was interviewed by Sonia, and Vanessa, the new team manager. The interview went well and they were impressed by the amount of knowledge and experience I had gained over the years, working there and within the Public and Private Sectors. Time passed and I did not hear the outcome of the interview. I eventually approached Vanessa and heard that I was unlucky, although my interview had been an excellent one. Later that afternoon I bumped into Mark at the drinks machine and guess what? He knew weeks earlier that I had not got the job and he had been told not to say anything. I was still on the merry-go-round of discontent. However, I was working with Sonia. Maybe, just maybe, things would change. Had Melanie interfered with the interview process in the hopes that I would return to her department.

No doubt, it is an everyday occurrence, people made scapegoats for other people's gain. I was made a scapegoat in the past by a manager who wanted his girlfriend to be promoted to team leader. When the relationship fizzled out, she told me the truth, in fact, so did he before I left the l Council. He was later to lose his job because he had someone else who wanted to destroy him and succeeded in doing so. In turn, that person lost something precious to him, his only daughter. I am sure there is a lesson to be learnt, injustice does not pay in the end.

It amazes me every day, the calibre of persons who become team managers, not necessarily by their competence in the job, but their ability to be downright nasty at times. The team manager who accepted a cake and then threw it in the bin, showing no regard for the person who gave it to him. When offered a new notebook, he told the person to 'stick it up your arse'. What makes a person think that it's all right to act that way? They would definitely not like it to be done to them.

The mis recording of work done to ensure that another person looks bad in the eyes of management. Management fails to question the statistics and the motives behind such performance ratings. At times, I wonder if they are too preoccupied with their own agendas, or worse again joining in to goad other persons to do their bidding. When I was on secondment, which by this time we came under the new department heading 'Customer Service Team', I took a phone call, nothing out of routine, only the call referred to a Credit Control query. I sent the details to my 'old' team by email. However, the reply back took me by surprise. It was clearly a case where all sense of logic and reasoning had gone flying out the window. The reply email, dated the 20th March 2008 at 16.17, was from Melanie, who had not hesitated in sending the email to an acting team leader:

I feel that I would have to let you have some feedback here. When you state can someone take ownership of this, I feel that this should have been done when the customer contacted you in the first instance. As you are on secondment, it does not follow that ownership is abdicated as you have a customer relationship.

Whilst I appreciate you may not want to deal with credit control issues, it is a customer that pays our salaries, and we should therefore deal with issues, not pass them off. You have the knowledge and access to do this.

Supporting each other is a great value to all teams.

Charming! With the greatest will in the world, how many eyes, ears and hands did she think I had? It was impossible to have feet in both camps. Thankfully, Sonia was not impressed and duly went to speak with Melanie on the matter.

Hell on Earth!

L ife continued as usual. The workplace had its changes, the Metal Support Team became the Customer Care Team. Sonia, the team manager, was moved to another section. I liked Sonia, she kept everyone under control. No one could override another team member.

I was moved to the 'In-life' team, which was another word for the 'call-centre' of the business, from the 21st April 2008 to 4th May 2008. I spent time going from there, on the customer care team, from 11th February 2008 to 21st April 2008. I learnt seven new databases during the process and worked for four different managers along the way.

On the 4th May 2008, I returned to the Customer Care Team on a permanent basis. I was dealing with manufacturers and dealerships. I obtained and maintained good working contacts with them, so all in all I was gaining further experience and knowledge throughout the business. I enjoyed the work, met the targets set – for example, 35 complaints in June 2008, 31 resolved and four on hold awaiting further information.

I received no customer complaints about me and no evidence was shown to me to prove otherwise that there had been any. Then out of nowhere, it was written on my job appraisal:

Alice has to change the way in which she handles customers. Recoveries at times can be a forceful role for customers that do not pay. Whilst dealing with complaints you need to stop and listen to the customer and fully understand their issues. At times, I feel you are trying to be customer-focused, but by not fully understanding the situation, and the impact the complaint makes on the customer results in poor feedback from the customers.

The report went on:

You look into issues and have always given me the information required to resolve more complex issues. I have also received good feedback on some cases from Sales, especially Stuart Brown, on thinking up solutions for key customers.

On a positive note, and taking into consideration feedback from both Credit Control and In-life, both teams have felt that you have handled the changes well, and during your moves to support the business, you have always continued to support your previous role until the issue is resolved.

Overall, I was happy with your performance in the customer care team for the months that you were supporting us and I do appreciate that you have worked in various departments during H1 for four different managers.

Personally, I was receiving good feedback from customers via emails and letters. I was puzzled. I was not stupid, let's be honest, you cannot please all of the customers all of the time.

I had been dealing with a vehicle issue for a customer, I shall call him Mr Michael N. He sent a letter stating the problem he had with his car, mainly water ingress in the rear passenger foot. His letter continued to list the actions that had been taken by the dealership to rectify the problem, to no avail.

Mr N continued:

At this point, Alice became involved as Customer Care Advisor on this case. Despite the further problems I am about to catalogue, I would like to praise the way Alice has dealt with the case on my behalf.

The outcome of the case was I worked with Alfa Romeo to provide the customer's vehicle with a replacement inside door strip pane as a gesture of goodwill. Later I was to negotiate a replacement carpet for the vehicle as a further gesture of goodwill from the manufacturer.

There were no letters, emails or otherwise of complaint. Someone had misread the letter he had sent or deliberately viewed it as a complaint. As time went on, I grew more aware the latter was happening.

What could I do? Nothing. Stick with the situation and do my utmost to supply the truth in every issue.

Sarah's close friend came as Sonia's replacement and God help me! Rona was hell on earth to work for and with. Her ruthless intimidation began as soon as she arrived at the section and no one missed the attitude she had.

When the team leader is a rotten egg, it is very easy for team members to take advantage and use it for their own gain. For the time being, the team were good, everyone got on and there was no backstabbing – that followed later when a member of staff was transferred from my old section, Credit Control.

I became Rona's prime target. I did not know why, however, months later she revealed her reasons when the damage had been done. I was definitely on the carousel, waiting to be pushed off at any minute.

The small glass-walled room beside the section became very familiar to me and a room I came to associate with a reprimand. The first time was to do with the case for Mr N. It was a complaint and it would not be tolerated. I explained otherwise, but I could see I had failed in my attempt. She said that I did not like her and she was not happy. At no time did I say or suggest that I did not like her, so where did her comment come from?

I was in the room to be criticised for the tone of my voice. She told me it was not suited to customer care work. I always had a good rapport with customers, I was never aggressive. What was the real issue, I wondered. With hindsight, instead of trying to continually explain I had done nothing, I should have insisted on her providing evidence. Was it a set-up ploy to get me running back to Credit Control, begging to be taken back? I had heard on the grapevine that they were struggling with replacing good staff and the debt was not being collected sufficiently. If that was the situation, why could they not have been straight and not acted like mindless scumbags?

The intimidation, accusations and criticism continued. The list became endless. It was reported to her that I used my mobile phone every day, only for a few minutes because I was a carer. I had been granted permission a few years earlier by Melanie. I asked her who had made the complaint. I was told that it was Credit Control. It could only have been Melanie herself. This was confirmed by Rona months and months later. Rona continued that Credit Control had a lot of work to do and I was upsetting them by using my phone, especially the new people. I asked the question, the new people did not know me, so how could they complain. I was not the only person to be on the phone.

Amazingly, they failed to see staff doing internet shopping or spending an hour or so discussing their social life. Where did I go wrong?

I was accused of not putting notes on the complaints database when clearly, they were there in black and white. Accused of placing complaints 'on hold' in error, which was the correct procedure for cases where further information was required. Accused of resolving complaints without the appropriate consent of the customers – no examples given to me to prove. Accused of working with the wrong business units to get results for customers – for example, going to Credit Control to discuss an excess mileage invoice. How ridiculous! I had worked in Credit Control for five years as a senior credit controller. Accused of internal and external complaints about my handling of cases – no evidence provided. She continued that colleagues had to help me with my workload – it was the first day back after my holidays! There were bound to be cases building up while I was away. She delighted in speaking aggressively to me, mostly in the company of other staff. At a meeting with a customer relations officer, she snatched my pen from my hand and accused me of failing to put notes on a case. The notes were very clearly done. I could do nothing right. By this time, I knew there was definitely a plan in place to usurp me. I use that word because the evidence told a different story.

My colleagues clearly noticed Rona's manner and tone with me and no more so when I got reprimanded in the presence of the team for asking Eddie (the company solicitor) in passing about the law regarding vehicle rejections. Rona was itching to know what we were talking about, so instead of asking me, she asked Tom directly. The outcome was a reprimand in front of the team. Rona was reluctant to carry out any training. I considered that no harm had been done, but I apologised to her in order to keep the peace. The team were mesmerised by her actions. We live in a democratic society and I knew Tom to speak with outside the workplace.

I dreaded my job appraisal with her. Into the glass-walled room again. How I felt sick at times. I wanted to leave, but sadly I always believed that people would come to their senses, realise the hurt they were causing, get to know the person themselves and not rely on gossip and other people's jealousies. I was somewhat prepared, it was going to be negative all the way. How right I was, there was nothing positive. I was deflated, I was never going to win, the hate was there for all to see. When I returned to the section, I was asked by an experienced colleague how the appraisal went for me. I told her. She shook her head and replied, "You do a very good job." My heart sank. I was being destroyed because of another person's discrimination.

The hatred continued. What did she want from me? I had done nothing wrong. I had a good reputation for getting the job done. What did she want the outcome to be? That I would hand in my notice? I was concerned at how far she would go. After all, there had already been a suicide in the office. I knew I was strong in mind and body, thank God, and I had a great circle of friends in the office and outside the workplace. Sometimes I think of the girl that worked in the office that was not strong in mind. At the time she committed suicide, managers spread the story that she was upset that she had been dumped by her boyfriend. The police visited the office a few times to ask questions.

Rona continued in her quest to destroy, aided by Melanie. Unfortunately for me, I sent an email to Credit Control and to their delight I omitted the customer's account number, although it would have been easily found on the system by putting in the vehicle registration. Well, Melanie had a field day. She sent an email by return to me, not only me but to everyone in Credit Control and the Customer Care team. Melanie was on a roll now. It got so bad that Rona advised me not to go to Credit Control without her accompanying me as a witness!

I got a respite period when Rona went on holiday. In her place was a very experienced team manager, Robin.

Rona had always insisted on checking my letters, tearing them apart, doing her crossings out with vigour and delighting in rewriting and copying her words, only for them to be crossed out again – she was correcting her own words. I duly passed my letters to Robin for checking. He could find no fault with my style of writing or my grammar. He was impressed and began to wonder what was going on with Rona He soon realised that it was a personal vendetta on Rona's behalf. Robin was not the only person to check my letters, three other people checked them too and surprise, surprise, could find no fault either.

The person with the vendetta will always find an accomplice, thinking that he or she will get a promotion for their 'good' work. It was early morning and we were busily organising our work for the day when I was asked a question in a very abrupt manner. So, I thought what the heck! So, I replied in the same appropriate manner. Why not? Like for like. I was getting fed up with being polite and professional. Most of these people did not understand the meaning but classed it as weak and timid. I was getting tired of the micro-managing, the constant criticism and the glass-walled room. They say there is nothing like a woman's venom. How true, though thankfully not all women are of that ilk. The phone rang and it was Rona asking me to go downstairs to the restaurant. What was it this time? You guessed it, another reprimand. This time it was for getting into an argument with my colleague and friend, Rachel. There had been no argument. I explained what had taken place and all seemed light-hearted. After all, we were friends, or so I believed. It was stupid, no one got hurt or insulted, and neither of us had been rude to each other. It was one person being abrupt and curt with another and the respondent being abrupt and curt back to teach the other a lesson.

Whatever, it did not fare well for either of us. Rachel did not get her promotion and left the company months later. Unknown to me until months after I had left the business, Rona l, the team leader, had entered this comment on my personal record:

Member of staff had a row with another member of staff today – had to be resolved.

There had been no argument between us, and even if there was, it would not have been the first in the office. Needless to say, I contacted HR, who advised me that the untrue comment could not be erased. My explanation was added to the record on the 7th February 2011 by HR.

There was to be no respite, Rona was determined to micro-manage me relentlessly. What was it all about? I was working hard, meeting targets. That was no good. Rona was on a mission to fault-find. In her quest to find faults with me, she was equally making herself look stupid. Such stupidity does not go unnoticed by other members of staff throughout the office. Her actions were erratic. One incident springs to mind. I was dealing with a complaint regarding a vehicle rejection and working with a supplying dealer to obtain a deal on the vehicle. Rona took this complaint from me, then passed it back to me a few days later. Then she took the complaint from me again, no reason given. In the meantime, the supplying dealer did make me an offer on the vehicle. I had done the deal. Rona passed the complaint to another colleague, Robin, who finally closed the case.

The monitoring stepped up a notch and my self-esteem and confidence lowered. There was the constant string of complaints about my work, how I was not meeting targets, the way I dealt with the customers was inadequate. Everything was recorded as the opposite of what was actually happening in reality. I was doing things so badly that I was to receive further training. I was instructed to watch training videos on customer care and handling complaints and various other training. Needless to say, it never happened.

I began to record my daily routine; workload, targets met, meetings, etc. I was going to be well-prepared if the situation got out of control. No one was going to get rid of me that easily. Rona then decided I was going to be given a mentor because I was so poor at my job. Jo was given the task. Jo became wise about what was going on. She found no errors in how I worked or how I conducted myself when dealing with customers. All she could say was, "You are in a no-win situation." How right she was. Jo was concerned. She spoke to Rona about her concerns. It was a total waste of time. Rona l continued regardless to have such a callous attitude. I began to realise that she had backing from someone more senior to her. Rona was going hammer and tongs. Nothing was going to deter her. Jo was shocked to see that Rona had recorded statistics for a period of when I was on holiday. The figures had been made up. This was not going to be the first time this was to happen to me. Surely senior managers were more interested in their staff and the workings of the office than that. The answer was quite simply 'no'. How far would they be prepared to stand back? I often wondered that. Would they be concerned if a member of staff was murdered in the office? Somehow, I think maybe one or two would be shocked, to others it would be a celebration.

I know that sounds harsh, but there was a real, could-not-care-less attitude. There had already been a suicide, so what! There had been a death of a young man at a wedding celebration, so what! I felt somehow uncomfortable at the time because staff were coming to me requesting that they wanted to in some way mark his passing, maybe a book of condolence, or leave lighted candles on his desk. Why ask me? I did not have the authority to make such a decision. The reply was straightforward. "But you know the right thing to do" – what a great compliment to receive. I advised my colleagues to seek advice from Melanie. She agreed. So there lay a book of condolences and lighted candles for Sandeep on his desk for a couple of days. I later heard that his parents treasured the book, after all, it was from his work colleagues. Senior managers made no comment as usual. Like an ostrich, they buried their heads in the sand.

My tortured work life continued. I was placed on an action plan – in other words, if my work did not improve, I was facing a disciplinary. The lies continued, situations distorted to suit Rona's devious plan. The written report stated that there had been a number of instances where customers, both internal and external, had complained specifically about me. What complaints? I was never told what these complaints were or who they were from. Everything was followed by doubt about me. It was all staged. I advised a customer to check with his insurance company regarding a recharge for a damaged windscreen. No harm in that advice, as some insurance companies make provisions for such a claim. Rona twisted the fact to read a 'damage recharge invoice', leaving a hazy question mark over the matter and its true details. If I asked Rona for help with obtaining knowledge, she ignored me.

I and the others realised that raising damage recharge invoices at the end of the vehicle contracts was an idle task, it wasted time and money, but then again, the business had to be seen to be doing the right thing. As a team manager once said, perception was important to the business. Damage recharge invoices were written off/cancelled if the recipient could fill the criteria of being a senior manager within RB. The words of one man still ring in my ears when he was asked to pay the outstanding invoice: "My wife is high up in the bank," and the invoice got cancelled. Other phrases come to mind: "I know your CEO, I'm going to speak with him." The invoice was duly cancelled. What a way to run a company! Managing it by threats from senior people and brokers (not all). Staff were frustrated by such a company practice. If these people did not have to pay, what about everyone else?

This could not go on. I brought her to the task at a meeting with her and, a senior manager. What was she playing at, criticising my every move, criticising the way I wrote my letters when no one else could find fault. Chris held down his head. They were both silenced. I continued: What age did they think I was? I had not just left school, it was not my first job. I had worked in local and central government. I had worked for the Price Commission. In that role, I had prepared written reports for County Court. Chris left the room stating that he had a meeting to attend. Rona became softer, even showed signs of tears and said, "I wish I had got to know you."

I felt sorry for her and accepted her apology in a way, but the time had come for me to move away from the section. It was a mistake I made, without realising it, I let my good nature rule my head.

Grade One, no way. Enough was enough and I requested an Informal Grievance Procedure to be put in place. I was concerned that there was no opportunity to raise concerns and issues in an open, positive environment. I felt subdued and could not operate as I would normally through fear of being viewed in a negative manner. I felt there was a bias against me be noticeable in the way management interacted with me. I doubted if the matter was being taken seriously. It took several attempts for a meeting to be arranged.

26th February 2009. 11:56
Good afternoon,
I appreciate that you are very busy, but I would like if the matter forwarded to you by Chris could be resolved as soon as possible.
I currently feel that the matter is not being taken as seriously as it should be.
Thank you

Regards.

***

Reply; 26th February 2009. 17:05
I am on leave at the moment but will look to try and catch you for a chat on Monday when I return.

***

5th March 2009. 11:19
I understand that Chris has spoken to you a few times this week regarding a meeting with myself. Please, Chris, can a meeting be arranged, you can appreciate I have been waiting nearly three weeks now.

***

21st April 2009. 12.59
Have you a new update for me please?

***

23rd June 2009. 15:14

From myself to Chris and Annie:

I am pleased to say that meetings have now been arranged.
1/07/09 at 3 P.M. – 4 P.M. with Sarah
2/07/09 at 10 A.M. – 11 A.M. with Rona
3/07/09 at 3 P.M. – 4 P.M. with Melanie

A meeting eventually took place with Senior Managers...I in turn was allowed to interview, or question would be more appropriate, the individuals concerned, those being Diane, Sarah, Rona and Melanie. It was hoped that they would realise that the game was up, there was to be no more snide planning of my downfall. Chris B's response was they had to be told, or more precisely Melanie. Chris H said: "If it ever got out what had taken place, then they would be taken out and shot." The outcome was I reverted to a Grade 3, with the promise that I could get involved with the upcoming projects.

New Opportunities Arise

There was a prize opening and I did not hesitate in submitting two ideas under the Bright Idea scheme. My ideas centred on training workshops and induction and training. As a result of this, Chris B advised me to speak with his wife Vicki about joining the project team. On speaking to Vicki, I joined the project team, working closely with Liz to produce the Skills and Knowledge Matrix.

Then, to my disappointment, Chris H left the company, apparently with a golden handshake, or so rumour had it. I felt that I was now back in a vulnerable position. I strongly believe that everyone needs a 'go-to' person, someone who can listen and investigate if necessary. If management is weak or devious, whichever matches, that leaves a large opening for bullying, intimidation, racism and other discrimination to take place. If management is strong, then those discriminations are kept to a minimum.

I was asked to design an award certificate. This was to be given to anyone who had succeeded in training. I sent a copy of this to Matt, who ignored it, so I went to see him after a few weeks, just to get an acknowledgement of receipt, nothing more. I was friendly and polite to him. He said he was waiting to speak to Vicki.

At the next meeting, Vicki advised, amongst other things, that a copy of the certificate should be placed on the project notice board by Sorcha. After the meeting, I went to her with the copy of the certificate and she blatantly refused to put it up. I was not going to argue with her. My heart sank. Nothing was really changing…but I kept hoping.

I accepted Vicki's invitation to visit the business centre in Leeds. The visit went ahead without me. Why I was left out I do not know. Nothing was discussed nor did I wish to discuss the matter either. I thought it was best to keep quiet. Vicki did have a tendency to forget things.

The project work continued. Faults in the methods of training arose and needed to be rectified, after all, company policy had to be adhered to. One such issue was the fact that senior staff were allowed to conduct job appraisals or 1-2-1s. I explained to Liz that this was not company policy and highlighted the pitfalls of such action. Liz agreed with me and said that she would speak to the Board. When she did, Liz told me that the Board said that no senior staff should carry out job appraisals, it was the duty of the team manager. We both agreed that seniors could be present at job appraisals if all parties agreed.

At this time, my new team manager was Janice, a slim, smartly dressed, black lady, who appeared to be everyone's friend. I discovered that there was a hidden side, the side that did not like being outshone. Months later I heard rumours that she was not the jovial, down-to-earth, nice person that she portrayed. With hindsight, maybe that was the secret of getting on. Janice always said that perception was important in the company's eyes.

Ah well, back to the story in hand. Liz had a word with Janice on the issue, then what followed was a meeting with Liz, Janice and myself, which I was not expecting. I explained the reasonings behind my findings and Janice explained hers. Liz backed down and Janice won the day. Whatever, I was basing my knowledge on company policy, so why was it difficult to follow? It never made sense to me. I guess once the rules were seen to be in place, then they could be broken on a whim.

The matter was not left there. Janice told Iain and bullying followed. Were they so stupid that everything had to be put on a personal level, or was it something else?

I had given a valid reason for suggesting what I did. I had backing from the Board and Liz, so therefore what was the problem. The bullying spiralled. I was forced once again to try and rectify the situation. A meeting was arranged to be attended by Janice, Iain, Paul and Jaysica, as a notetaker, and myself. Again, I stressed that my ideas/suggestions were centred around the project work and that no one was being held back or to suffer. The solution was to provide training. I was wasting my time. There was a hidden agenda by Janice, and this was confirmed when I was called to a meeting with Linda, the acting CEO, and Janice. Linda seemed puzzled as to why the meeting was arranged. I was with the Project Bloom team after all.

Janice was going to a banquet out of the matter. At the team meeting, she said that she would be doing my job appraisal and Iain would be doing everyone else's. It was not fair. I did not deserve such treatment from either Janice or Iain, now I was being discriminated against. I realised that nothing was going to change, people did not like change. Many could not comprehend that legal requirements in any business were required. Maybe some people would say I was stubborn, others would applaud my efforts to reorganise a failing system. Do I regret my efforts? No, not really. I believed in doing a job well, not in half measures.

It became more and more apparent that people did not want to change, had their own egos to support, too thick at times to understand the logic and good sense for the business. All was to become apparent to me in the not-too-distant future.

Around the Office in a Whirlwind

By now, I had worked in every department possible. Credit Control, worked on all the ledgers, with the exception of the corporate ledger. Metal Support Team, Customer Care Team, In-life Team, back to Customer Care Team. Vehicle Contract Amendments, Vehicle Administration. Helped cover phones for various other sections too.

The introduction of Personal Development Plans did nothing to change the culture of the office. Again, it was all based on perception, to be seen to do the right thing. These plans became tedious, and the contents largely ignored by management. "What would you like to do? Where do you see yourself in a year's time?" Answers to such questions were ignored. I remember I had a well-constructed plan, only to watch in dismay as my team leader crossed everything out and then my Personal Development Plan ended up in the bin. It goes without saying, but I knew there was no hope of my knowledge and skills being rewarded. Oh! I was going to be given lots of work, moved from one department to another to help out when they were struggling, but that was it.

Each day brought new challenges for me. It was becoming apparent that as long as I carried out my work, then I would survive. I was an achiever. I was not being selfish in my attitude. I included the team. My ideas could be accepted or rejected, providing that it was all for the good of the business.

I had to do something. Informal Grievance Procedure.

Another Change, a New Direction

I moved to the Vehicle Contract Amendments section and quickly settled in. I was delighted to be away from Rona, although her attitude changed after that meeting. It was 'come to me if you need anything', accompanied with an array of smiles.

My new team leader was Annie. It was a very pleasant time. It gave me time to breathe, but the work was not really my cup of tea, but I worked hard as always and met the targets set. I heard on the grapevine that Credit Control were struggling with the job of bringing in the debt. New staff had failed to rise to the occasion. I was asked if I would help them out. Again, my good nature came into play and I agreed to do so. However, I did so on the proviso that I could work from my current desk on Vehicle Contract Amendments. That proved to be no problem, so I worked for two months on the ledger and as always hit the target. I was rewarded with a bouquet of beautiful flowers from Melanie. I graciously accepted them. Did I do right by accepting them? It was a question I would later be asked. I felt it would have been rude of me to reject them. I was puzzled and concerned – was this person secretly plotting against me and promoting my downfall? What were the reasons behind the plan? Diane, Sarah and later, Rona blamed Melanie for what was happening to me. In the meantime, the team continued to thrive. I achieved 'Employee of the Month' and an award for the highest call-taker.

Sadly, the situation was to change. Annie announced that she was leaving and her future husband was leaving too. I always felt that Annie did not fit in as a team leader, not because she was not good at her job, but she failed at being a puppet for someone else. Annie did not carry out my job appraisal, stating that she was not qualified to do so. I had more knowledge than her. Staff were moved around the office and I was to work for another team manager, Janice, on Vehicle Administration.

Keep Going

However, someone somewhere was placing a fly in the ointment, and a large jar of ointment at that! The continuous criticism, without evidence, is tedious and distressing. My proof? Rona changed her attitude towards me. Oh! If there was anything she could help me with, she was available. When I had put the cards on the table at that meeting with her and Chris H, she knew the game was up, and indeed he did too.

I decided to test her honesty on the matter. I sent an email to her, the email highlighting the problem that sometimes, at the end of the contract, vehicles would be in another place, other than where they should be, and that was at the returning depot. Was there a way a final check could be put in place in the system, as one computer system recorded the vehicle as returned when it had not? Please can you advise me, Rona, is this correct? Rona was very accommodating in her response. "Of course," I was delighted to read, "that's a great idea about putting a final check in place and Pam and I will definitely investigate how we can go about doing that." It continued: "There is a mismatch, as one source records matured status and one doesn't. It's a bit of a problem but we know about those cars so we can still chase them back." Finally, "Thanks for all your ideas, we will definitely see what we can do about them!!!"

A year or so later, I was researching the culture at RB Why? Because of a comment made by The General Secretary of the Trade Union:

"It would be a waste of time taking RB to a tribunal as they have the lawyers who would destroy you."

My research took me through viewing loads of cases from past employees. Some appeared minor, some far more serious, meaning whereby it affected the individual's health, the most inconsiderate and callous of issues brought about by management's inability or arrogance to deal with the problem/issue/situation.

Human resources are no longer trained and qualified to manage these everyday occurrences in the workplace. No, they would rather pay expensive lawyers and destroy lives instead. What happened to staff loyalty? It works both ways. How many of these so-called 'troublemakers' or square-peg-in-a-round-hole clichés were in fact experienced, qualified, hard-working employees, who finished their careers with reputations in tatters? Their only plan and thought was to correct a wrong that was done to them, obviously by a lead leader or manager with a problem themselves, unable to deal with a person with an asset or assets higher or better than their own.

Two tribunal cases stood out for me. They left an impression of why on earth were these issues allowed to get out of hand? Why there was so much opposition to arrive at a fair and understanding finale?

The first case centred on a lady who had time off work to care for a sick child, the other case was clearly an issue of racial discrimination.

Both of these employees lost their cases, both cases would have been managed differently many years ago. Tragic really.

Many cases never air at a tribunal, with most employees walking away to start again somewhere new, with renewed hope in their hearts to rise from the ashes of rejection, broken confidence and low self-esteem.

Soon after I arrived at RB with high hopes myself, I noticed a male employee working at a desk in the Credit Control department. He appeared to be working on a project not connected with my department. He worked most of the day in silence, clicking backwards and forwards from one screen to another. Now and then he would be interrupted by a member of management, asked a tirade of questions, these questions promptly were answered and off the person went. After a few days, I realised that he was assigned to special one-off projects, which were executed professionally.

But it also came to light that he had requested promotion to a higher level of salary for his expertise. Senior management continued to refuse his request and he finally gave up and produced his letter of resignation. He had secured a position at another corporate institution and he appeared to light up with his newfound worth.

To his dismay, on handing in his letter of resignation to his superior, he was called into a director's office for a meeting. Looking puzzled, he went. On his return, he was so disgusted and appalled that on tendering his resignation he was subsequently offered an increase in salary and promotion. Why the reluctance not to come to this agreement earlier? He was obviously worth his salt, as the saying goes.

Have we reached the point of saying that in technology we have made great strides in human relationships we have taken steps backwards?

I continued to make suggestions about staff training and development, all under the banner of Project Bloom. Heading the project team was Vicki. I sent an email to Vicki regarding a follow-up suggestion. Janice called another meeting, an event that occurred on a frequent basis, but of course, it was a sense of power. Janice began the conversation, asking why I had sent the email. I duly replied that it was connected with the project work. What Janice said next was a revelation, 'Why did I think that Vicki would speak to me?' Simply, the answer was I was part of the project team. Her response was that Vicki was too busy to talk to me. Vicki could easily have come back to me when she was less busy. I was the writer and sender of the email, or was that asking a little too much maybe?

I was never going to get into an argument. I would certainly state my case, and I always believed that good dialogue was always beneficial to all parties. Janice looked at me. I was facing a losing battle and I knew it too. Unintentionally, I was upsetting the culture of the office. I was later to realise I was upsetting the culture of the business. Throw away the rule book, the law, the regulations, and the respectable, acceptable thing to do.

Janice proceeded to inform that I was – her words – "Banging my head against a brick wall and that the company was never going to change." She continued that she had worked for the company for eighteen years and the company was not going to change. The rant went on that 'nobody knew me…did Richard (a director) know me?' Well, considering he had spoken to me now and again, then he knew of me. He did not know what I liked to eat or what my hobbies were, so on a familiar basis, he did not know me…But what was the point of her question?

The conversation and the matter were left there and we went back to our desks. Power is dangerous in the wrong hands, and certainly in Janice's hands. On the 11th October 2010, I had my 1-2-1 with Janice. *'All went well, or so,'* I thought. She told me she had a few comments to add. Okay, but why not discuss those few comments with me there and then? At 4.45 P.M. I received an email from her stating that I was insensitive to other people's needs and that I undermined a manager. I replied to the email:

I have read the attached, please can you give me some examples, then we can cover the points together and I can learn from them.

I am very surprised, as in all my years of working I have never been known to be insensitive to other people and always known for being positive. Thanks, Janice.

Regards,
Alice.

***

Janice, 17.10 on 11th October 2010:

This is not a problem. When you book the pep time in, we can discuss at the same time, no problem at all.

***

Also, that same day, at 16.51, email from Janice:

Good feedback given from the contact team for the number of calls taken. Went through the list of messages which were taken by you, as I was curious to the reasons why some of them on the list you could not answer, as you have the experience of working within the In-life team and covering the phones before. You have advised due to the volume of calls coming in you had to start taking messages so as to have less impact to the customer waiting.

What the hell was going on? The above comment related to the Pro-Drive event that took place on the 8th September 2011 near Warwick and I volunteered to assist on phone duty for the day. Those of us who did cover the phones were advised to pass over any queries left at the end of the day to the In-life team (term used for the life of the contract) and those of us with more experience of the business were to help other staff with queries. At the end of the day, I passed over five queries that were left. The next day Janice brought me into a meeting room and reprimanded me for leaving five queries when clearly, I should have been able to deal with them. My response: The phones were busy, skeleton staff in the office, and I was advising colleagues on queries…The majority of the office was on a Fun Day!

The emails continued to flow between us, however, it was becoming very clear what the game was on Janice's part.

Myself:

I am very concerned about the comments regarding 1-2-1 as these have not been discussed with me. I want to explain how the situation arose. I joined the Project Bloom team and discussed some observations I had made with Liz together, we discussed the problems and the solutions and of course, the matter was left with Liz to raise the matter to the Board…I did not undermine anyone's authority in the matter and made this very clear.

What I did suggest was in the interest of the business and 'in confidence' with Liz. At no time did I make a complaint. I stated my observations. I was taking an interest in the business and taking an active part in the project group, to assist in some small way to 'finding a way'. I was demonstrating a very positive attitude.

*I would also like to stress that a **no** time did I object to Iain doing 1-2-1. At no time would I be insensitive to anyone's feelings. In fact, I have been told by previous managers that I tend to be too considerate towards others.*

I would also like to stress that my observations were based on training and knowledge I had gained in previous employment and therefore thought they would be welcome by the business.

Unfortunately, the matter was treated as a sleight and therefore led to unnecessary hurt feelings by yourself, Iain and me.

Neither have I incurred any argument with any member of the team.

I hope this clarifies the situation.

Regards, Alice

***

Reply from Janice:

This is not a problem. When you book PDP time in, we can discuss at the same time. No problem at all.

***

Reply from Janice:

I am very surprised that you have emailed me with your concerns and not taken the opportunity to book your PDP time where I have advised that we would discuss your concerns. I feel that your comments would be more beneficial discussed face to face rather than over an email. As advised previously, please look in my calendar and book some time in. I am conducting interviews Thursday and Friday, but it is pretty free next week.

***

15th October:

Alice and I have had a conversation and discussed the comments I made. We are both going to work together to ensure that the matter does not reoccur, and we will take it as a lesson learnt.

What lesson? Only that I was to keep quiet, to be seen but not heard unless it suited.

The situation was ridiculous. I pulled out of the project work and Janice told me to destroy my Personal Development Plan and start again in 2011. The plans were designed to be an ongoing file. Why did I have to discard it?

You Don't Need Halloween!

We are surrounded each day by witches and bitches, planners and plotters, each one deciding how they can systematically destroy someone's career…And the problem is they manage to succeed.

It had been the brainchild of Janice's that 360 Degree Feedbacks were to be carried out on everyone in our team only. Great, fine, no problem if you know what you are doing. How do these 360 Degree Feedbacks actually work in practice? There lies the big problem. Janice nor her deputy did not have a clue.

The 360 Degree Feedbacks were an excuse by staff to demolish each other, with no strong understanding of what these feedbacks were designed to achieve. 360 Degree Feedback is a system or process in which employees receive confidential, anonymous feedback from people who work around them. This typically includes the employee's manager, peers and direct reports.

I was in the process of doing my work when I was asked to go to one of the meeting rooms. My instant reaction in my mind was 'what now?' I was still finding the constant invitations to go to a meeting room tedious. It was always a 'destroy you' moment. I went to the meeting room, my stomach churning as I went. What was I going to be told? What accusation was going to be made? Who would be in the room? The meeting rooms had glass doors and walls so I could see clearly that Kiranne and Janice were in the room. Instantly I knew it was going to be about something I said or did.

I was told to sit and I was advised that a 360 Degree Feedback had been done about me by Kiranne and no one else. Management had a bad trait of turning a person's positive skills or attributes into negative ones. The onslaught was going to be tough. It began with being told that I was approachable and friendly to members outside the team, therefore appearing welcoming. It continued: I displayed a bad attitude with the team by deliberately being argumentative and awkward, creating poor team morale and a bad atmosphere amongst everyone…How?

It went on and on…as currently within the team there have been many occasions where you imply that you are a team-orientated player, however, get treated as an outcast by your colleagues. Yet, you yourself will never participate. Examples of this are contributing to the team's 360 Feedbacks. You held the meeting yet never completed anybody's or asked for your own to be completed. You choose to ignore all the forms sent over to you.

Like hell was I going to complete or hand anything over to Janice. I had made it clear to her that no way, I was not going to do so. No one wants to be 'set up' by a team led by a person who is unable to rise up the ladder on their own merits. The trick was to de-merit the person who was mostly liked and respected and who happened to be good at their job.

Possibly the next attack will give a clear indication of why I chose not to take part in the 360 fiasco.

Yes, I had switched off to an extent, to the extent I wanted to get on with my daily routine and disappear at the end of the day unnoticed. There are still times when I want to disappear, times when I wonder have, I lost my brain, my self-worth, and then I bounce back and do my writing, which I enjoy. My hobbies and interests are plentiful. Sometimes, I feel I should live like a recluse to keep people happy. I have a mixed bag of friends, the genuine ones who like to hear good news and are with me in bad times. Others who go green at the gills and spit feathers if I am rejoicing and delight in my sadness. I am pleased to say I have rid my life of those types. They only get inside the head and destroy.

Back to attacks. At team meetings, we had to give a 'chuff' figure from one to five. On the occasion in question, I said three, and why not? I had lost Alan, a devoted boyfriend of three years. Sadly, he had died unexpectedly of a heart attack, the white gold and diamond engagement ring replaced in the box to be revisited now and again. I was not feeling great. How cruel and bitchy for that time to be mentioned to me. I was cornered. No warning and no backup plan. Professionalism was in short supply. Each day was a return to the school playground, although I do not remember it being this bad. I was sitting next to a professional bully. Kiranne was capable of getting people to 'ride' with her. She thought she was going to get to the top, but then no one likes a 'backstabber'. Do it once, it is easy to do it time and time again.

The meeting continued. Clearly watching 'Big Brother's House' on TV was where she had got her training; a reality show with contestants falling out and bitching about each other. It was the main topic of conversation on the section, together with the programme 'EastEnders'. "Making out that you're an outcast…clearly singled individuals during post issues and communicated in a patronising way when showing examples of Welsh posts and adverts." Was there to be no let-up? What was she talking about?

I was accused of being deceptive/manipulative, taunting at conversations and I failed to take part in a quiz, which was not surprising as I had not been given the information. However, she failed to mention that I had single-handedly won first prize for the team when they failed to know the answers to the quiz! She told me that she did not like me. Okay, that was her choice. I did remind her that she invited me to her wedding, and when Alan died she and her husband gave me two rose bushes as a gift to be planted in memory of Alan, which I did and both roses are thriving in the garden, one purple and the other pink…so why the change in attitude? Turning to Janice she claimed that she did not know why she was in the meeting room in the first place saying stupid things to me. I got the measure of what was happening. Kiranne had sided with Janice on the promise of 'getting on'.

No one was going to set me up. I had had enough of this living hell and childish pranks. I went immediately to speak with Garth Kelly, the new director on the matter. I told him that I had received no warning of what was going to take place and the outcome of the meeting. He was disgusted and advised he would speak directly with Janice that afternoon. Amazingly, Janice was on annual leave in the afternoon, but he caught up with her the next morning.

I saw Janice out of the office accompanied by a lead leader from another section, Alexia of course. Garth would have wanted a witness to what was being said. Was I trying to change man-management skills in the office? In a word – yes, not for power or glory, but to safeguard the wellbeing of everyone. I was always aware that employers had a duty of care towards their employees. Business is business and pleasure is pleasure. If you need to sack someone, then do it for the right reasons, genuine evidence and fads, and follow employment law. To leave work at the end of the day with a clear conscience, or am I being a tad naïve?

Did my action pay off? I don't think so. Most team leaders stick together despite the truth or integrity. Coupled with jealously of the individual leads to a dangerous combination. Alexia was not an easy person to read. She was emotionless on the surface, and there was no passion in anything she did. She did what she had to do and went home to her widowed father. No more was known. To an extent, I felt sorry for her.

Fill Your Boots

When people want to be bitchy they fail to listen to the detail, digest the information and arrive at an intelligent decision.

August 2011, the CEO, made the remark at a coffee morning session that we should 'fill our boots' as regards taking the opportunity to join training courses. I applied for sponsorship to do career coaching. My request was rejected, the reason being that finances had been allocated for the year.

Are you wondering why I chose that latter subject? Because it would have been a step into the training department, rather than just doing project work centred on training. I was not deterred. I began the Diploma course in my own time and with my own money. However, I was aware that three members of the team, were allowed to go on a two-day course to London with an overnight stay in a London hotel.

I received permission from Sam on the 1st September 2011 to seek the help I needed to enable me to do the course. I asked a few team leaders to complete a questionnaire and of course explained the reasoning for the request face to face, Alexia being one of them.

On 24th October 2011 at 16.42, I received an email from her and she put Janice on copy:

I have now had time to look at the questionnaire which you gave me this morning. To be honest, I don't really understand what it is asking with the question, "Would you consider 'The Power of Communication'?" What is this in relation to and what are the bullet points underneath? Also the question, 'Do you have other topics in mind?' For what? The final question on the back I find a little insulting and rude. Clearly, you are aware that we have Personal Development Plans and that we have an internal Training Team.

Alexia was on a roll, determined to hit out, regardless of how stupid it made her appear. She continued:

If this questionnaire is all about 'The Power of Communication', unfortunately, it has failed. It does not clearly communicate what this is in relation to or questions that can be answered. I'm not sure what you are expecting to get out of this or for what reason, as that was also not clear.

My immediate thought was here we go again! Yes, I wanted to move up the corporate ladder. I was supposed to play down my abilities to keep some people happy. Even now I can smell bitchiness a mile away! How many people can say that? I guess most of us. We can spend hours trying to ponder and wonder why someone is treating us with a certain amount of contempt. I have given up on that waste of time, after reading a recent article stating that if someone is hurtful and bitchy it is because that person has a hidden agenda. Sometimes we can figure out their reasoning and sometimes it is impossible. My advice is don't waste your precious time.

I wanted to keep the peace with Alexia. On the 27th October 2011, I replied to her and put Janice on copy:

Hi Alxia,

I know that I have spoken to you regarding your email.

Just a few points to clarify any confusion and to avoid any misunderstandings.

I am, as I earlier stated, doing a course in career coaching, which is a progression from the Management qualification I have obtained. I appreciate that the normal process is for team managers to request training packages through our internal training team.

However, what I am doing is not to replace anything within the company…It might only serve as a supplementary resource, but the main aim is to enable me to carry out the practical aspect of the course.

I understand PDP and the processes that are in place

The leaflet was designed as a general marketing exercise, not aimed at the company…I have since changed the wording.

I would have liked if you had come to me and offered constructive criticism, then we could have understood each other better.

Regarding presentations, I have been given permission by Sam to carry them out, and I have stressed quite clearly the purpose of why I am doing them.

I hope my email clarifies the situation and stresses that there was no intention on my part to insult anyone.

To date, though, I have received some really informative feedback which will help me immensely.

Kind regards,
Alice

Alexia did become friendlier thereafter and left the company a few months later.

People can be sucked into another person's agenda quite easily.

By now, I was given advice by various persons; to lie low, be quiet, come to work and go home at the end of the day and stay quiet in between…don't shine out!

I was told by two colleagues that 'they are out to bring you down, but not to let them'. Wow! A tall order, but would I be able to continue? Already two years or more of battering. Why did I continue to stay? I knew by now redundancy was on the cards for all of us, and I was not going to lose out on redundancy pay.

I spoke to Sam, to explain the latter situation. He told me that two managers had gone to him with concerns. His advice was that they did not understand and it would be best if I concentrated on the course outside of work (although what I was learning would benefit the business. Maybe that was the problem). I had given my plan, my reason, and the parallels. I was asked to explain the word parallel. He explained that he had allowed me to do presentations, but that was all. I felt that he was in the middle of a situation and did not know how to handle it effectively for all parties.

There was a plot to halt me in my tracks. I was questioned by Janice: Why was I doing the course? Where was I going to get my information from? How would I know that the information I was presenting was correct?

I began to realise more intently that I was not working for a major business, but an institution without sound business management principles, but made up the rules as they went along. How long was I going to last?

The man-management style was easy to follow: If an employee was positive, change to negative and vice versa, depending on the needs.

By Now…There Was No Going Back

I wonder what you are thinking by now. Are you thinking how stupid I was for 'sticking things out'? Are you thinking…how sad! Or are you thinking I did not want to be beaten? Stubborn? Wanted to prove something? None of those things. I had proven myself over and over again. I guess I was trying to prove who I was. Why? I don't know. I had worked there a long time, I had an excellent reputation, the continuous supply of emails and letters was the evidence.

By now, there were talks of the possibility of the business being sold. Redundancy? Who knows. Okay, take my pay out and run like hell out of the place. I wanted a good pension to survive and to be financially sound.

I made the decision to stick it out, go with the flow, but rightly or wrongly, I wanted to be ambitious! That was it, that was the main factor. I was ambitious! A trait I knew I had, but I never really realised how strong that trait was. I was an achiever! I had always been an achiever…that was why I was getting the treatment I was getting. Any job I did, I did it well and as Janice said, the more difficult the task the more I came alive. The amazing statement, "You are an icon! Do you know why you are being kept back?" You know, those moments when someone says something to you and you're aghast, speechless. You know what you want to say back, but somehow the words will not come out of your mouth. What is holding you back? Fear? Scared of hearing the truth? No, it is fear of being upset, even more, the urge not to cry in public, the fear you would never be able to stop. The fear mainly is not wanting to be hurt even more.

I did get to work on project teams, I did manage the feat of setting up the Performance Boards, not a popular subject with staff because it made everyone accountable for their work. I was tasked with that job, getting the staff behind the scheme. The scheme was good, it kept a track on the work targets, who was working and who was not. But because of the bullying culture within the office, it was used as a tool for that purpose. If a task was not completed fully by a member of staff, then their work for the day was not counted. It gave the impression to management that the person had spent the day doing nothing, they had nothing to show for their day, it was as simple as that.

Anything and everything could be twisted to suit the requirements of unscrupulous team leaders. Senior managers were not interested. If you were being set up, so what, you must have earned it. I endured mental bullying. I met targets, I surpassed targets; I began to keep records of my daily workload. Charlotte whispered in my ear, "They are trying to destroy you, don't let them."

Deborah said, "You are from a different background."

Keep going, don't give up, don't let them get to you, think of other things, plan other things, think of my family, think of Mum, think of Alan. Dress up, put on the high heels and dance the night away.

There were some good things at work; the treasure hunt away from the office, the Think Tank sessions at Millennium Point in Birmingham on the 4th December 2009. Staff was asked to send in ideas to a director, for further improvements in the business.

So, on the 7th February 2009, I sent mine in too. I was told by Janice that I did not know enough about the business. So, on the back of that statement, I went all out to learn even more. I shadowed senior managers to gain knowledge. Won a prize on the 'Bright Ideas Board'.

I asked if I could 'shadow' the Training team. Well, that was an experience. May 2011, time allocation was 09:23–16:12. The session lasted ten minutes, sitting in a group. Wow! Shannon the team leader, had a bee in her bonnet, big time. I did not know what her problem was, never did find out, but I knew she was dangerous in a subtle way. There is always a sidekick on a team, the one who will do anything the team leader requests of them, be it good, bad or indifferent. Shannon had one of those. I can't remember her name now, it began with an E. She piped up, "We are trained managers on this team," spitting vindictiveness at the same time. I said nothing. The atmosphere was already hostile.

I got fed up and began to take control of what I wanted to do. I made the decision I was going to do the career coaching course. I was passionate about people getting on in life and enjoying what they did.

A Woman's Scorn

Believe me, women can hate with a vengeance. Thankfully not all. No doubt there are men that can hate with a vengeance too.

So, okay, I wanted to do things right in the workplace, towards people and the business. I strongly believed that both these agendas could work side by side. That was not the case. I was told that the business practices were never going to change. Most people had agendas, their wishes and dreams, and I had mine.

I was told, I was warned, but I was determined. I had my camp, they had theirs. I arranged a meeting with the senior union rep, a pleasant man with a bushy beard. God, I was getting to dread those glass cube meeting rooms – cold to touch and cold to feelings. The meeting was quick and short. He listened to my brief tale of woe. His reply was equally brief and gentle. Using his hands, he gestured to me. "You are up there, they are down there. You're too clever for them." And so ended the meeting.

Oh, now what to do? I had been told not to use 'big' words after doing a presentation to some staff. I cannot remember what the word was. As far as I was concerned it was an everyday word. Sometimes, I think in life it is hard to win. People who want you to act professionally, people that do not want you to. People that want you to be good at what you do, others that don't want you to be. Do you follow your heart or your head? I guess follow both equally and, if possible, stay in the middle of the road.

I decided to stay middle of the road, keep my opinions to myself, basically, lie low. I mastered the act, did my work, went home, chatted to colleagues. I ignored staff shopping on the internet for the latest fashion item, ignored a colleague discussing his on-the-side car sales business.

We had our usual team meetings, we learnt the art of stating the above five on a 'chuff chart', giving the indication that all was well with the world for each of us. Anything below five and you were given the third degree of what, why, when and how, with no remedy to the problem. I have just had a flashback: On returning to our desk after one such meeting, I heard Kiranne say to another colleague, Jaysica, "I did not get her this time, but I will get her again." What on earth was her problem? I had been to her wedding, we exchanged gifts for special occasions. Was she promised the golden prize of promotion? Was she being enticed by someone pulling the strings? There was only one person that appeared to fit that description: the team manager.

I was on the ball, I was alert and determined not to be beaten, and so began the chess game, her move, my countermove, all tactical, while being polite and professional with each other. The team manager Janice did not want change, that was her agenda. As she said to me, "You're banging your head against a brick wall. I have worked for the company for eighteen years, and it is not going to change." She continued, "Does Richard know you?" Richard was a director; did he know me? Interesting. Well, I had given him a rubber. Does that count as knowing me? Why him? What was the point of the question?

I was kept busy around the office, sent into various departments to handle backlogs and issues. I pulled out of the project work, which began to have no real meaning or purpose for me anymore. I had given up. Employment law, Discrimination law, fairness and doing things right were of no use.

Definitely There Was No Going Back

There was no going back. The snake was spitting venom, and the battle was taking place. I had my 1-2-1 with Janice on the 13th October 2010. *'All went well,'* as I thought, however, she told me she had a few comments to add. At 4.45 P.M., I received an email from her that I was insensitive to other people's needs and that I undermined a manager. Why did she not mention that at the meeting? Why the afterthought? She knew I was working with the project team under the heading 'Project Bloom'.

Over the years I have learnt that it is quite easy to be criticised with no real justification. I had organised fundraisers, section 'parties' for Ede and other occasions and became a 'big sister' to other staff, training them and encouraging when I could. Please, do not get me wrong, I am not claiming to be astonishing or out of this world, I am a human being after all, but I am wise enough to admit when I have done wrong.

The next 1-2-1 soon came around December 2010. This time I was advised – if that is the word to use – more like told to scrap my PDP, Personal Development Plan, for 2010 and start again in 2011. There was no way I was going to scrap it! My achievements were not going to be disregarded for anyone!

On my return from holiday, Janice asked myself and Tim to step into the meeting room. Here we go again, only this time it appeared I had a partner in crime. Poor Tim…The job was only temporary. He was looking forward to the day he began training as a police officer. I hope he got his wish. I was astonished at what she said. The workload had built up while I was on holiday. Tim was helping in another area of the business, and with the greatest will in the world, how could he manage to work in two places at once. She told Tim that it would be easy enough to get rid of him, but more difficult to get rid of me!

What was happening? Had all sense of logic gone out the window? Tim was furious to say the least. I was not particularly happy either. For goodness' sake, how about informing people of the latest business updates on their return from holiday?

This was not a good management practice. It was bullying. I hurriedly sent an email to the Finance Director with the details of the meeting. I do not know what the outcome was.

I decided at that point that enough was enough. I was getting disheartened with the whole sorry situation. I remembered what Mark had told me: come into work, lie low and go home at the end of the day. Surely at my age, I should have been thinking of retiring! Excuse me! What age did he think I was? Heck, he knew what age I was, and no, I was not nearing retirement age. There was a whole lot of mileage in me yet, God willing of course. I knew what he meant, I was not nineteen, an age preferred by my employer.

There was to be no let-up. The battle was on. By this time, Janice had another accomplice, Ivan . I had to sign an agreement to hold me to meeting targets. If targets were not met, I received an email to explain myself. No one else appeared to have such an agreement, except Tim, but even then, I was not sure.

The attitude on the team was mixed. Kiranne was a prime troublemaker, she knew how to work with people. The sneaky one that goes behind people's backs and complains about things when there really is nothing to complain about. Always the person to try to get someone into trouble and create doubt in someone's head. This factor had a profound effect on me. To this day I hate when someone goes behind my back to complain instead of discussing a matter with me directly, both professionally and personally.

13th January 2011

Dear Alice,

I refer to your letter of 13th December 2010 in which you invoke Stage I of the Group's Grievance procedure and now write to invite you to attend a meeting on 18th January 2011 at 2.00 P.M. at Brindley place, meeting room tba.

The purpose of this meeting is to discuss the issues raised in your letter. I have been identified as the Grievance Hearer as I am independent and impartial having had no prior involvement with the issues raised in your grievance.

I remind you that you have the right to be represented under the Group's Grievance policy either by a union representative or by a work colleague.

At the meeting, you will be given the opportunity to outline the issues relating to your grievance and to bring forward any matters which you consider relevant.

You should refer to the group's grievance policy for further information, Please confirm that you will be able to attend on the date and time stated.

Yours sincerely,
Head of Technical Services

January 2011 – Grievance Hearing

Minutes of Meeting Template

Minutes of Meeting convened under the Group's Grievance Procedures at Brindleyplace room 7.6.02 on 19/1/2011 10.00 A.M.

Alice Kenny has been requested to attend a meeting to discuss the issues raised in their formal grievance submitted under Stage (I, II) of the Group's Grievance Procedure.

The parties introduced themselves and the notetaker who will provide an abbreviated note of today's hearing for agreement.

Alice confirmed that she had both read and understood the Group's Grievance procedure.

Alice confirms that she has received the invite letter and received 3 days' notice. Present an independent and impartial manager and has had no prior involvement in the issues surrounding this grievance.

Alice was informed that she had a right to be represented and she stated that she understood that right and confirmed that an is Union Representative is in attendance. Any contribution that the representative wished to make at this hearing would be welcome.

The purpose of this meeting is to ascertain the employee's grounds for raising a grievance.

Alice was asked to outline the issues raised in the grievance.

Alice explained she felt that due to <u>previous experiences she could not give her viewpoints and put forward her ideas in the business</u>. She explained that she felt she was being viewed as <u>negative</u> and <u>not taken seriously</u>. Alice felt that there had been <u>hostility</u> toward her over the last 6 years and <u>her freedom of speech</u>

89

had been taken from her. Alice felt that she had not received recognition for her contributions and now had lost her confidence.

Alice described several instances over the last 6 years involving different managers which had led to Alice feeling that people had an agenda against her. The instances were discussed along with communication between Alice and managers, opportunity to contribute, engagement with managers and feedback.

Alice was asked what she wanted to achieve from the grievance hearing. Alice explained that she wanted her character cleared so that she could be viewed as trustworthy and can work well with others and an opportunity to be taken seriously. Alice confirmed that she gets on well with her current line manager, Janice, and has no real issues with her.

It was suggested Alice worked with Janice to develop communication and influencing competencies.

The union representative suggested drawing a line under the past and work together moving forward.

Alice confirmed she was happy to draw a line under the past and work with her current line manager and to give and receive constructive feedback.

Comments on Alice's recent 1-2-1 were discussed and Alice felt she had not been given the opportunity to discuss them with her line manager in the 1-2-1. This was to be discussed committed to discuss this with Alice's manager.

Trevor suggested, and it was agreed, that he will arrange a three-way meeting with Alice and her manager to agree a way of working together going forward, including feedback, development and communication. It was also suggested that a mentor may be useful.

Both Alice and her representative were advised that a decision would be made following investigation and that decision would be confirmed in writing.

Meeting concluded at 12.00.

***

25th January 2011

Dear Alice

I write following our meeting on 19th January 2011 convened in accordance with the Group's Grievance Procedure.

I trust that it will be apparent from this letter that I have spent a considerable amount of time investigating and responding to your concerns.

Please find below details of my investigation into your grievance.

My Role

As you are aware, I am Head of Technical Services and as such, I did not have any involvement with the issues surrounding your grievance. I am therefore independent and I have approached this grievance from an impartial perspective. I have also been supported by Policy and Advice Services.

Your Grievance

Your grievance related to your feeling that you were being viewed in a negative manner and not being taken seriously over the last six years. You felt you had not received recognition for your contributions and resulted in a loss of confidence.

Investigation Process

Your initial grievance letter was dated 13th December 2010. Following this, I wrote to you 13th January 2011 and you attended a formal grievance meeting on 19th January 2011. You were offered the right to be represented at this meeting and you were represented by Ludwig.

It was agreed that I would arrange a three-way meeting with yourself and Janice your line manager. The object of this meeting was to agree a way of working together going forward including feedback, development and communication.

My Decision

During the meeting, you explained that you felt you were being viewed as negative and not taken seriously. You felt that there had been <u>hostility toward you over the last six years</u> and your freedom of speech had been taken from you and that you had now lost your confidence.

You provided me with examples of the above and described instances involving previous managers. <u>You did confirm that you get on well with your current manager Janice</u>. Following the examples, you raised we had a discussion about your communication with managers and your opportunity to contribute.

You explained that you were happy to draw a line under the past and I, therefore, conclude that this element of your grievance has been withdrawn.

You also raised the fact that you had not been given the opportunity to discuss comments on your last 1-2-1 with your line manager. I confirmed that I would raise this personally with your line manager which I have done.

You explained that what you wanted to achieve was to have the opportunity to be taken seriously and to be viewed as trustworthy. In order to resolve the situation and plan for moving forward, I suggested that I hold a meeting with yourself and your line manager. The aim of this meeting was to agree on ways of working together including feedback, development and communication. I also suggested that a mentor may be useful and this is worth exploring.

We held the meeting on 24th January 2011 at 2.00 P.M. and we all agreed that you would take part in a 360 degree feedback exercise that would assist in developing your PDP. Janice will support you in this exercise. I also highlight that you should ensure your 1-2-1 meetings and documents are a true reflection of your feelings so that issues can be addressed and not allowed time to fester.

Following the meeting, you agreed that the matter has now been resolved. I believe that we have come to a satisfactory way of working in the future and the actions put in place will prevent a recurrence of this situation, therefore I believe we can close this matter.

I trust that this letter responds to all the points which you have raised, but if you are unhappy with my decision, you may raise an appeal under Stage 2 of the grievance policy. You should refer to the group's grievance policy for further information. Any appeal should be made to me in writing and within 14 calendar days of receipt of this letter.

Yours sincerely,

The meeting was a farce really. The notes did not indicate much in the way of gathering information but rather seemed to be more like mediation without one of the parties present. Why did he suggest a meeting with Janice in light of the allegations against her? Why did he not question the allegations of hostility and deal with the matter in a constructive way?

The union rep who was interested in my case was quickly promoted and advised to pull out of the union, so ended that. On the HR file, it was noted that 'I wanted to draw a line under the past and the grievance withdrawn'.

Informal Grievance Procedure

The date, 19th January 2011 after eight years and three months, I was reaching the point of no return.

I stated my case and how I felt, provided the evidence as you do. He was sitting on the fence. He said I lacked confidence. At this, the union rep interjected. Alice does not lack confidence, she is articulate, knows her job, all the evidence is there. All evidence is also there too, showing clearly acts of bullying and intimidation. There was no real solution, only that Janice could do a 360 Degree Feedback report and hopefully, the unpleasant working environment would cease. Did I believe that? Sure, I did. After all, we were all adults. I did want the hostility, intimidation and victimisation to stop, the sniping and back-biting to cease. All I wanted was to be dealt with in a fair fashion without prejudice, and where feedback was required, I requested it be delivered in a constructive manner so I could learn from my mistakes without fear of reprisal. I wanted to do my day-to-day job functions with the opportunity to work to my potential with a chance to progress and better myself.

On the 7th July 2011, Kiranne had snapped at me, once too often. Enough was enough. I was unhappy about her conduct and I told her so. But Kiranne was a woman not going to let go. She sent an email to Janice criticising me, accusing me of not asking her if she wanted a drink and looking at her monitor! How the hell did she think I could read her monitor when I was not near her desk? A meeting was set up with Janice, Alexia taking notes, and myself. Kiranne had a notebook with her, which twenty-five minutes earlier she was busy writing notes and talking to Janice. It was another set-up; the discussion was ridiculous. I had asked if she wanted a drink, I had asked all the team. I had only walked past her desk; how could I possibly have seen what she was typing? She continued that I taunted at conversations. I did not know what she was talking about. I spoke to the, Head of Department. He duly spoke to Janice on the matter.

I was beginning to be micro-managed and felt I could no longer communicate with the team, only if I had to. I was laughing with a colleague from another team, Matthew I was asked by Janice, was I on drugs or had I been on the pop! I chose to ignore the remark. Amazing how she noticed me but failed to spot her team playing word games and talking socially throughout the day. The environment got worse. If I met my targets, I was promptly told that I had not met the timings. Contradictory, no evidence comments were put on 1-2-1 reports, such as targets currently met, September 88%, October 97%, November 98%.

Comment: Closer attention to detail required to meet 98%. Lateness, currently arriving late for work, September 2 times, October 2 times, November 4 times, no dates given, and no reasons given. Comment: Need to arrive at work ready to start at 9.00 A.M. starting 14th November 2011. The date I was put on an Action Plan. Inconsistent on targets, timekeeping, rework, lowering morale of the team. Oh! I was watched, my every move and who I was talking to. The system crashed, she was ready and willing to criticise.

Please, please, was this ever going to come to a halt? Would the merry-go-round stop? Was I ever going to be released?

11th February 2011
Group Human Resources
Manchester
M3 2 LAQ

Dear

Thank you for your email regarding the comment and the action taken on the 'PeopleSoft' database.

I am relieved that the very stressful and unpleasant experience of the past six years is hopefully coming to a close.

Although the matter is nearing a close, I have had to endure character assassination, my personality curbed and I was denied my freedom of speech. These are extremely serious factors.

I would like to know, how the Bank are going to compensate me for the latter and loss of earnings?

I have made it known several times during my Personal Development meetings that I am very interested in staff training and development. I would like to pursue this line of interest; I do hold a management accreditation, which includes personnel, training and development management.

In view of the treatment, I have received within the company it would it be a good idea if someone, such as myself, took on the role of monitoring culture and to ensure that all 1-2-1 and job appraisals are conducted in the correct manner.

To also ensure that managers realise that they have a duty of care towards their staff, equally staff have a duty of care to their employer. Also, improve communications within the business. I have been told that the company is 'big' on perception – but this has to be used in the correct way. In March, I am giving a presentation to the team on 360 Feedbacks.

I am willing to go on a specialist course for life coaching in business; in fact, I have seen the details of a course I am interested in.

I look forward to hearing from you, in the hopes that the matter can be well and truly resolved.

Yours sincerely,

***

Letter

Dear Alice

I write further to your recent email in which you enclosed a copy of a letter dated 11th February 2011 that you sent to Group Human Resources. I apologise for the delay in responding to your letter.

I was pleased to see from your letter that you confirm that the unpleasant experiences you had previously referred to were coming to a close. As a result, I have undertaken a review of the content of your letter which I understand relates to a grievance at a meeting on 19th January 2011. Following this meeting, confirmation of the findings in relation to your grievance and also held a three-way meeting with yourself and your current line manager to agree a way of working together in the future, with a particular emphasis on feedback, your development and communication in general. I was also pleased to note from your email that Janice is providing you with good support.

Whilst I note from your letter of 11th February that you acknowledge that 'the matter is nearing a close' you have asked for clarification of how the Group is going to compensate you in relation to your grievance and for loss of earnings. I understand from a review of the grievance statement template that you completed that you had requested compensation in the section entitled 'What are you looking for as a result of raising this grievance?'

I was advised that in your grievance meeting you just wanted the matter sorted out. Following a review of the minutes of the meeting, there is also no mention of any discussion concerning the loss of earnings/compensation. We believe that both you and your representative at the meeting agreed that you were happy to draw a line under the past and as such he concluded that this element of your grievance was withdrawn and concentrated on working with you and your line manager to develop you in the future.

Following a review of Trevor's decision letter, he concluded that following the three-way meeting with Janice the matter had been resolved and he believed that you had come to agree on a satisfactory way of working in the future, with actions put in place to prevent any future recurrence of the situation that had led to you raising the grievance. There was no further mention of the requirement for compensation and it would appear that matters had been resolved to your satisfaction.

Finally, I am pleased to see and acknowledge from your email that you hold a management accreditation that includes personnel, training and development. I also acknowledge that you are giving a presentation to the team on 360 Degree Feedback. In my opinion, your desire to be involved in staff training and development is something that you should discuss with your manager J as part of your ongoing performance and development discussions.

I trust my letter responds to all the points you have raised.

Yours sincerely,

***

The Royal Bank
London
EC3M RC
4th March 2011

Dear

Thank you for your letter dated the 23rd March 2011; however, I feel as a 'victim' of the company I feel that the matter has not been treated as seriously as it should be.

I understand that you are not aware of all the incidents that took place, some too painful to relate, and on the advice of the union representative, I was told to reduce the number of incidents to be mentioned at the meeting.

Prior to the meeting, the union representative asked me if I had ever done anything to upset any of the managers – the answer was a definite no. I thought long and hard and remembered that someone had submitted an anonymous complaint about a manager to HR. I was on leave on the day in question and had no part in what took place. I am extremely concerned. Have I been blamed for the incident?

I mentioned this matter, but he advised against speaking directly about the matter.

The team manager in Credit Control at the time, stated that Melanie did not like me because 'I could think on my feet'.

Please can you find the answer for me? I need to know why I was subjected to such aggression and bullying. Why have persons named Melanie as the instigator?

I am very interested in being part of the Training and Development Team; I know that I can bring knowledge and experience to the team, to be proactive within the team. I will be discussing this, as I would want to make the move now.

As my progress within the company has been hindered by discrimination and bullying behaviour, I wish to pursue my goals. I am interested in a course, centred on business behaviours, which would benefit the business. Of course, I would benefit also, and restore my confidence in my employer if I were to receive financial support and together with senior management support.

I have carried out two presentations, the 360 feedback and finding a way – how we can improve as a business.

Outside work I am also involved in projects as a member of the Finance Committee within the church I attend (persons are chosen by the parish priest, not voted nor can the individual volunteer).

Independently, I have organised dances to raise funds, and recently I have written a book about the history of the church and the surrounding area. The book will shortly be completed at the publishers and released for sale. It has been suggested that I write another book – at the moment I do not have the time, but who knows, maybe one day.

I appreciate that you have taken the time to consider the situation, but I do need your help further in answering my questions.

Yours sincerely,
Alice Kenny

Well, Here I Go!

Well, here I go! What was I to do? I was determined to get to the bottom of things, I decided, so on the 27th August, I sent an email to the Group Human Resources requesting all information held on me by the company. I was extremely worried that someone had accused me of a horrific wrongdoing. I remembered Martin trying to 'blacklist' Melanie by contacting HR with a list of her shortcomings. Was I being blamed for playing a part in what happened? Had he used my phone to make the call? Okay, I knew there was a variety of discrimination going on. But this was something serious. This was not going to end well. I had to survive, I must keep going.

Each day I laughed, talked, and joked with my circle of friends on the train, met for lunch, as I did with the close friends I worked with. On nearing the office, a friend would ask if I was all right. Why? was my reply. Well, you go very pale the nearer you get to the entrance. Be careful, she would warn, don't get into ill health whatever you do. Wise words.

Outside of work, my social life was great; many acquaintances, and close friends. My special friends, four of us who knew each other from senior school, and our families got to know each other well. We came from Catholic and Irish backgrounds and shared similar interests. Luckily, I had hobbies; cooking, sewing, and tennis. Interests included the cinema, theatre, and music. My passion was dancing. On a Friday night, I would get enveloped in the world of Ceroc, Salsa, jives, the Twist, the Waltz, three hours of being twirled around the floor to my heart's content, always made special by dancing with the noted good dancer in the room. Sometimes Johnny Carroll would be there, a well-known local comedian and singer. Danced with him a few times. He was a lot older, but he had a youthfulness about him.

The information duly arrived. All good except for an entry on the 'PeopleSoft' system, with no evidence to support the accusation. The accusation: Underperformance, not delivering on targets, failing to be acknowledging complaint, bad call monitoring – poor customer service, and finally: had a row with another member of the team, had to be resolved. And guess what? No backing evidence and I hasten to add neither did I. There was no row. On the 7th February 2011, I replied via email to deny the charge of having a row. As a result, the comment was added: *She disputes that she had a row with another team member. It was agreed her view would be noted on PeopleSoft.* Why were these comments put on the system? Unless it can be proven. Why was an unproven allegation included in PeopleSoft?

I followed with a letter.

Dignity at Work

Many rules and regulations, always good to be seen to have them within the realms of business, gives the impression that maybe things are okay…maybe not perfect, but okay.

The danger lies in the wrong hands, persons who twist those roles to their own agenda, persons also who simply do not understand the complexities. Whatever the reason, it can lead to a daunting, frightening, and mental torture for an individual.

Well, the 'Dignity at Work' was written out concisely, no flaws, no uncertainty. It stated the Royal Bank is committed to creating a working environment in which individuals are valued for their contribution and can develop to their full potential. All employees have the right to be treated with dignity and respect at work. Harassment or bullying of any kind will not be tolerated. Employees should always act in a professional manner. Employees should bring to the attention of management any incidents of bullying or harassment of colleagues, customers, or suppliers that they have witnessed or experienced.

Bullying and harassment are unacceptable and can have a significant effect on the wellbeing, engagement, and motivation of an individual. The Group, therefore, aims to: create a climate free from bullying and harassment. Ensure all employees feel confident to raise concerns of this nature. Provide a clearly defined procedure to support the resolution of complaints effectively and in a timely and sensitive manner. Wow! Bullying and harassment are regarded as serious misconduct under our disciplinary procedure and may result in disciplinary action up to and including dismissal in serious cases. The Group may also report the incident to the Police.

The Stages of the Procedure are explained in lengthy detail, starting with the Stages of the Procedure, firstly, the Formal. An Employee raises the matter with their line manager in writing. Where the complaint is against the line manager, then the matter should be raised with another line manager. Then an investigation should follow, with a decision made based on the findings. Second Stage, an Appeal, if an unsatisfactory decision is reached, then Discretionary Appeal, whereby the decision of a Business Director or designated delegate is final.

So, there we have it, and the route of no return, informal discussions proved short-lived. It was now time for me to forge ahead. I had a determination to prove…prove what? I had nothing to prove. I could not erase who I was. I had an Irish background, that was not going to change.

I had noticed that when I was dating Alan, there was a change in attitude. Alan was English, his father Scottish and his mother Irish. A little bit of Welsh and I would have had the British Isles covered! I would have been untouchable, maybe, maybe not. All I know is I got a little respite from the torment.

I digress back to the business in hand, following the stages, followed the guidance for the person making the complaint. Preparing the statement, personal details, background to the complaint, specific allegations and witnesses and any other information to support the allegations.

Finally, a full guidance in detail of what to do, responsibilities of the persons taking part and clearly what the Group's responsibility was. Ensure the procedure is clearly explained. Support the parties in attempting to resolve the matter informally. Make confidential counselling available by contacting the company's 'Lifematters' team. Ensure that confidentiality is preserved as far as is appropriate.

What is the difference between a dignity at work complaint and a grievance? The Dignity at Work Procedure is used for complaints relating to bullying and harassment. A Grievance is a complaint about the effect of an unfair decision or a process or policy.

On reflection, the policies state that employees do not normally have the right to be accompanied by relatives and friends. I get the point of that – people close to the person are going to be biased. Not allowing legal advisors – I do not understand the reasoning. Surely, it would prove effective for the obvious reasons.

Triggers, Targets and Colic!

I was battling on. Keep on going, do not give in, keep a low profile. Maybe the lower I keep, the less they will notice me. Who was I fooling? I did my work, stayed late to finish a job, continued to assist other sections when required, continuing to meet targets, sometimes well over and above the requirements. I had no choice. I knew in my heart that things were not looking good.

However, I wanted to survive if possible. Redundancies were looming for the whole department. An American company had pulled out of a deal to buy the business, but another company was interested. I needed to hang on. I was not going to forgo my redundancy pay-out.

I felt disillusioned. There was no hope. Management was indifferent, 'I'm alright Jack's mentality. But somewhere I thought there had to be someone different, someone who took pride in their man management skills. No one came to light.

Sadly, I was to see my one ally leave, very abruptly, with an apparently massive pay-out. I felt Chris was batting for me. Now I was lost. I had no senior manager to turn to, I was on my own.

I struggled to go to work in mind and body. I did not want to go there. I was sick listening to stupid squabbling, ridiculous meet meetings, playing stupid quizzes, and listening to how targets were not met, with every stupid obstacle put in place to hinder meeting targets.

It was worse than being at school. I was no longer working alongside adult professional colleagues, but morons incapable of thinking, making rules and processes up as they went along. Their only interest was television, soaps being the main interest, and bullying. I knew who my enemies were – two coloured ladies. Heaven forbid if asked about world affairs and who the British Prime Minister was, was surely met with blank expressions.

My health was showing signs of stress: 27/07/2010 – sore throat; 23/11/2010 – upset stomach; 14/01/2011 – colic; 08/03/2011 – cold; and 16/05/2011 – upset stomach.

I had reached the trigger points and the road of no return. Part of me was giving up, but I wanted to last the distance, the day when the company ceased to exist.

Confirmation of Written Warning

J anice had caught me. I had to go with the flow as best I could muster. There was something not quite right. I got a verbal warning on the 2nd June 2011 to watch my sick leave. The letter stated:

Following our meeting on the 2nd June which convened under the Group's Disciplinary Guidelines. You were given at least three days' notice of the meeting, your right to representation was explained to you and you declined to be represented. Alexia was also present at the meeting to take notes. I confirm that you were given a Written Warning for failure to meet the Group's required standards. Namely that you exceeded the trigger amounts being 5 occasions. This warning will remain in force for a period of 12 months.

I enclose two copies of the notes of the meeting. Please sign and return one copy to me within two days. A copy of this letter will be held in your personnel file for the length of the warning period and a record also maintained on the HR system.

During the warning period, any further breach of the Group's required standards (which include but are not limited to performance, attendance, timekeeping, breaches of procedure, conduct) may lead to further disciplinary proceedings.

You should also be aware that during the period of the warning future sickness absence may lead to loss of Group Sick Pay, the loss of the right to self-certify and bonuses/incentives may be withheld.

I would remind you of your right to appeal against the decision. Should you appeal, you should do so as soon as possible, and preferably in writing to The Manager (Appeals), HR Policy and Advice Services...

Any appeal should be made within 14 calendar days of receipt of this letter. Please clearly state the reasons for your appeal.

Yours sincerely,
Janice

The meeting did not achieve any satisfaction on my part. I stated that my cause of sickness was brought about by stress. Grievances were not resolved. I tried in vain to win Janice on my side by saying that she was helping me!

Was it normal practice to issue a written warning in such circumstances? Could the company prove that I was treated as any other employee?

Where were the return to work completed forms?

A letter duly followed dated 20th June 2011:

I refer to your letter received on the 9th June 2011 stating that you wish to appeal against the decision to issue you with a written warning.

Further to our conversation on Thursday 16th June, I write to confirm that you are invited to attend an appeal meeting on 22nd June 2011 at 2 P.M. in meeting room 10.03.01.

The meeting will be held under the appeal section of the Group's disciplinary guidelines which can be accessed on the Intranet under human resources.

During the meeting, you will have the opportunity to discuss the grounds for your appeal.

I remind you that you have the right to be represented at the meeting either by a union representative or by a work colleague.

Please contact me by the 22nd June to confirm that you can attend on the date and time stated.

Yours sincerely,

***

Meeting Room 10.03.01

The 22nd June 2011 at 14:30. Present: me, Alice Kenny, Head of Strategic Partnerships (Appeal Hearer) and a notetaker,

The usual preliminaries were carried out and the meeting continued.

In accordance with the Disciplinary Appeals Procedure, Alice was asked to put forward the issues they would like to be taken into consideration and given the opportunity to make representations as to the grounds for appeal.

HS – We will not discuss the Grievance as I believe the grievance for bullying has been resolved. When looking through the notes, the return to work for the sickness, there were no notes related to stress caused by Grievance.

AK – I did not mention the stress/grievance as I was fed up repeating myself. The absences for colic and the cold were both stress-related.

HS – On the 27/07/2010, was this sickness related to stress?

AK – Yes it was stress-related as there was an informal grievance that was ongoing at the time.

HS – On the 23/11/2010, was this sickness related to stress?

AK – No.

HS – The fact that you were near your trigger points was discussed/documented in this Return to Work. Why did you not discuss the reasons behind the sickness at this point?

AK – HR had been made aware of the reasons for the sickness.

HS – Is this documented?

AK – No.

HS – On the 14/01/2011, was this sickness related to stress?

AK – This was the instance where I had colic which was linked to stress and was again due to the ongoing informal grievance raised 19/01/11.

HS – On the 14/01/2011, was the sickness related to stress?

AK – This was when I had a cold which was linked to stress and was again due to the ongoing informal grievance.

HS – So the Informal Grievance had not been resolved.

AK – No, there were a lot of issues, and there had been ongoing issues for 6 years. I had gone to the point where there was resolution and was discussing ongoing issues with management. However, when he left, I feel there was nowhere to go. So, a Grievance was raised in January and I also responded to a message from management regarding instances of bullying in the workplace. Things from there seemed (spelt 'seamed' in the report) *to progress and a resolution was made early in May. I feel I can now speak to Janice regarding any issues.* (How wrong I was to try and get her on side, so to speak.)

HS – What changed between March and May?

AK – I feel I can now speak to Janice .

HS – What changed though?

AK – Janice got to know me and now seems (spelt 'seams' in the report) *to listen and understand me and not listen to gossip.*

HS – On the 16/05/2011, was this sickness related to stress?

AK – This was an upset stomach possibly from something I ate.

HS – From our discussions, I can see some correlation between grievance and sickness but in the majority cannot see a link. Is there anything you would like to add?

AK – I have discussed the issues to the limit and want to move on.

HS – There are 3 instances where the absences were due to an upset stomach. It is hard to determine if these were stress-related.

AK – The instances where I had colic and a cold were stress-related.

HS – There is no medical evidence that cold is related to stress…

(Needless to say, that was an incorrect statement she made. Why did she not check it out?)

…But can understand that colic is related to stress.

AK – I went through a very tough time and would not want anyone else to have to go.

through a similar experience.

HS – Do you understand the sickness policy of 14 days or 4 occurrences?

AK – Yes.

HS – And the Return to Work reasons do not show that these instances of sickness were stress-related.

AK – It was a very tough time, but has been much better since May.

HS – We will adjourn now, and I will speak to HR and we will arrange a follow-up meeting tomorrow. Meeting adjourned 14.50.

Adjournment

Following the adjournment,

As only one of the five return to work documents mentioned stress, which I can see is a direct correlation to the time the grievance was raised and that in all five of the return-to-work meetings there is an opportunity to disclose factors relating to the sickness. There are notes in the return-to-work documents clearly explaining the trigger points and consequences.

Confirmation of Appeal Outcome

STRICTLY PRIVATE AND CONFIDENTIAL
24TH JUNE 2011

I write following the meetings on both 22nd June and 23rd June 2011 after your letter we received on 9th June appealing the decision to issue you with a written warning.

You were given at least three days' notice of the meeting, your right to representation was explained to you and you declined to be represented.

I now confirm that the decision of the appeal hearing was that the decision to issue you with a written warning is upheld.

The reasons for my decision are as follows:

When reviewing and discussing your Return to Work (RTW) documentation, only one out of five RTW Interviews did you mention stress, this is the sickness between the 14th January and 17th January 2011 and you had the opportunity to discuss relating factors to the sickness on every occasion, which you did not.

I enclose two copies of the notes of the meeting. Please sign and return one copy to me within two days.

I should remind you that my decision is final.

Yours sincerely,

That settled that. What the hell! I decided that I was going to come out on top. They had the power and they were going to use it. They were not interested in resolving any matter, they were not prepared to view evidence. I was discriminated against on racial and ageism grounds. Jealousy was a part of the treatment too. I was good at my job, and believe it or not, I can to this day still prove it.

I had my allies, the colleagues that knew what was going on, the ones that encouraged me to hang on in there, not to give up. I am afraid that is easier said than done but bless them, I knew they meant well.

I was on my way to New Street Station relishing the idea of catching the early train if I walked fast enough that is. My thoughts were broken by a cheerful hello. It was Ian. Ian worked on another team, but I had worked with him for a short period when I had been asked to help that team. Ian had plans. He wanted to be a writer and was in the process of writing a crime novel. I wonder if he achieved his ambition. I like when people do. Ian and I got into a short but meaningful conversation. He asked if I was okay. I replied not really, but I will keep going. We suddenly stopped walking. He looked straight at me and made a poignant statement. I hope you have plans, Alice, they are trying to get you out. If you can hang on in there, do not let them. You are too clever, and you know what is going to happen to the business. Alice, I have plans too, it is good to have them. We continued walking. I went into the station, Ian briskly walked to his bus stop.

I made it to the platform, the train was coming to a halt. This evening there were more people than usual, all rushing forward to get on the train. It was standing room only. I was huddled into a corner by the doors, saved from being squashed completely by a tall dark-haired man holding onto the handrail that was positioned from floor to ceiling. He smiled and said I will not let you get squashed. I returned a smile.

I wanted to cry, I wanted to run away from the office as fast as I could, I wanted to be free. The whole situation had gotten out of hand. I was me. I was who I was. Nothing in the whole wide world was going to change that. I was in a nightmare, relieved when it was time to go home.

Invites to lunch with workplace friends and my new group of friends from the train was a pleasure. I could no longer hide how I felt, apparently it was clear.

Those glass-enclosed rooms became once more a familiar place, beckoned into them so many times. Tom and I were made to sign contracts agreeing to meeting targets. Did others have to sign these contracts? I doubt it, as we never heard them discussing them.

Tim was as fed up as me. He was mesmerised by the tactics of management and bewildered by the antics of some of the team. He eagerly looked forward to handing in his notice and a career in the police force. I hope he achieved his dream too.

After the contract signing and Janice telling Tim that it would be difficult to get rid of me, I kept a log each day of the work I had done, what came in and what was actioned. I continued to work as requested on various sections to lower backlogs. I was now desperately trying to keep a low profile. I gave no opinions or suggestions at meet meetings, I let the others get on with it with that task. It was getting more and more like the school playground than a professional business.

Janice was watching me very closely; who spoke to me and who I spoke to. Back into the glass room on the 11th November 2011 for another reprimand. What now? Bit by bit I was being destroyed, my character and personality being taken away from me. Well, here we go, another round of criticism. She had noticed that I was talking to Lesley, how Lisa had spoken to me, then Andrew. Another day I was not logged in on the system when I should have been. My monitor had 'crashed'. That was nothing new in the office. Luckily, I had a witness – Barry from the Maintenance Department. She requested that I send her an email at the end of every day stating what my work schedule was the following day. Why, I wondered, when I was now being told what to do by another senior member of staff, Iain, another Ian.

I sat and listened to her and did not question her. I did not have the strength to respond. I would not have won anyway. I was being micro-managed; everything was being watched and scrutinised. If I met my targets, I was told I had not met the timings. If the photocopier was playing up and I could not take copies of documents, then my work was not counted for the day. I worked eighty fines in a day, could not photocopy the attached documents, then I got a zero rating for the day. The game was over!

Where Are Your Thoughts?

Where are your thoughts and what lies behind them, contradictions, contradictions? Ah! But who am I? The good team player? Alice is currently covering the phones for the Contact Team and is doing it on behalf of the whole team. Alice has shown a real team-orientated attitude by doing this. Alice is enjoying learning new processes and the information whilst doing this cover.

How long is a pause? Never been timed, never seen anything in writing stating how long a pause is supposed to be.

'We identified that Alice could leave long pauses when speaking to a customer without letting the customer know what she is doing, which can be frustrating for the customer on the phone.' No examples given. I do not know about you, but I always like to be shown evidence. Come on, let us be honest, the devil is in the details. How many customers did I frustrate?

'I have listened to some of Alice's calls whilst sitting next to her and she displays a confident attitude when speaking to difficult customers.'

'Alice has been working on Climate Scan on behalf of the team and has contributed to the sessions with Chris… Alice comes back into the team to update us with any actions or new processes to be followed.'

Wow! I remember being nominated to 'spin the wheel' on the prize board as a reward for good customer service. However, I can't remember what the prize was now, partly because I made a conscious decision to block out a lot of things. Experiences that I do not want to relive, although I will not forget the experience if you get my drift.

Can a person be all things? I doubt it. I remember a blind gentleman, Miles Hilton-Barber, coming to give a talk at one of the usual company presentations. This time the conference was held in the hotel next door. We walked into the room to the strains of 'We Can Be Heroes'. Miles was amazing, blind since his twenties, he had a zest for life. He went exploring, he had undertaken a host of extreme endurance events, he was a world record-breaking adventurer. He sledged across Antarctica to track across huge expanses of desert on foot. His fearless acts combined with his managerial experience make for rich, inspirational talks. His achievements are breathtaking and leave all listeners spellbound. He spends many hours travelling, doing motivational speaking. This statement about him is true. *'Miles has the ability to get everyone engaged in the room; he can make you laugh, cry, inspire you to reach your dreams.'* There was one statement that really stood out for me. He said, *'No one can be two people. If a person achieves success outside of the workplace, then that person will achieve success inside the workplace.'*

'Alice has remained a very stable and valuable member of the team, she has shown concern and consideration for the customers and the business, well done Alice.'

'Alice also has a lot of responsibility outside of her daily role; she is heavily involved in project 'Bloom' where she has been doing some fantastic work with the team board and feedback from meetings. She has also taken the lead in producing the Fulfilment newsletter by chairing meetings and taking time out of her day to ensure that the paper is completed monthly. Overall, Alice is doing an excellent job in managing the work queues.'

'Alice has taken the responsibility of the Vehicle Admin Board. She has displayed loads of energy, and passion into this which is really nice to see that we have yet another member of the team so customer-focused and wanting Vehicle Admin to stand out amongst the rest.'

There was a new project on the horizon: 'Customer Experience'. It was to be known as such. Staff who were interested in taking part had to create a business manifesto and to place the document in the appropriate box to be viewed by senior management. The closing date arrived. My manifesto was the only one in the box. The closing date arrived and there was no mention of the outcome. I sent an email to enquire about the outcome. Oh. I received a reply that there had been a delay. Each manifesto was placed on the large noticeboard for everyone To view. Unfortunately, I was not one of the chosen few to join the new project board. What was lovely and encouraging was the feedback from the staff. A manager told me that my manifesto was the real deal, not the others, as he said a statement, *"'Enjoying going for coffee' did not improve the business."* Janice wrote, *'She has still shown total commitment in bringing the experience to the team. Great start to your new roles, Alice. I am truly looking forward to working with you in 2010 to bring all your ideas to life.'*

Oops! We have a hiccup. Caught using the office phone for a personal call. I asked permission, I got permission to call the garage about my car from the senior manager. Well, what can I say really? Nothing said to those staff shopping online for clothes, concert tickets and cars! No, of course not, only those being watched, are watched.

'Alice can come across as negative and I do not feel that she understands this. I have explained to Alice that she needs to apply her experience to the company process, values, and competencies. Alice will be the first person I will ask to cover other areas of the business phones and she will always offer to help with an incredibly positive attitude.' All that in one paragraph! It went on. *'I overheard her tell colleagues to email the person currently carrying out the process when I really would have liked Alice to be able to deal with it as she has the knowledge of what to do. This would have shown me more of her team spirit.'* Gosh, what was going on here? How could I be in two places at once, meeting a target of 100% each day, continuing to raise my profile within the business?

I was not going to be beaten. I attended business awareness days and achieved a 'Bright Idea Award' for introducing Training Workshops. *'Alice has performed well throughout Q4 and this can be seen by the reduction in her ledger from £1.6 million to £1.08 million. She is deeply knowledgeable of both the business and its processes and this stands her in good stead.'*

'Alice failed to meet her targets on the 30th July.' Nothing said about being called away to assist a colleague.

The rot was beginning to settle in. It was becoming difficult to stay in control. *'Alice has not met her daily targets again.'* No mention of the other tasks I was given or the times I was told to stop doing something and do something else. Then the ultimate, having to ask someone to check that my worksheets had been signed off correctly. Janice was winning, but I had to persevere somehow.

I had been 'tipped off', as they say, I knew what was going on. I continued to keep a record of my daily workload. 765 dealt with, 821 dealt with, 172 sorted, 242 sorted, covering phones, etc., etc.

I continued to raise cost-effective solutions; not requesting unnecessary V5 vehicle documents, a substantial saving to the business. By grouping vehicles under each manufacturer, then making one call to each manufacturer for supplying dealers and in some cases contacting the supplying dealer requesting information again on a group of vehicles.

I was advised to build understanding and trust. What trust! Sure, I was losing trust fast. The knives were out, someone was working on others. Janice had the power and she was using it. Her criticism was rampant. I was accused of making assumptions about other persons' views. Insensitive to the thoughts and feelings of colleagues. Creating boundaries and barriers between people and units. Attempting to gain influence by undermining or attacking the position of others, and finally, reacting to symptoms rather than understanding underlying causes. I am lost! What was she talking about? But then, when you want someone gone, it is easy to bribe and encourage others to follow your plot.

Why did I agree to sign the stupid contract that she had set up? Based on a 360-minute working day, 60-minute lunch break and 60 minutes for chat, toilet, etc., 30 seconds for an MOT update, address mismatch; 1 minute, 30 seconds.

The evidence of stress was showing. I lost my voice and my review was cancelled. I was now put on a performance warning for not meeting targets, customer complaints and lowering team morale. The performance warning was ridiculous, only to be issued when a rating of '1' or '2' at an annual or half-yearly performance appraisal was given. I was a 3 at the last half-yearly appraisal. Okay, lower than it had been, but due to the restructuring of the business. The rest of the performance form was not completed. I had given up. I was no longer interested in the business. I wanted to do my work, go home, and wait patiently until the business finally ceased to exist.

The End Is Nigh!

Eagerness can be damaging depending, of course, on where it is placed and what the eagerness is involved in. Eagerness is great when it is involved in goodness. All aspects of the job are covered. But eagerness in revenge, to damage someone or to lower a person's self-esteem is rushed and tiny elements of faults are highlighted.

The wrong date is put on a letter, the aggression shows through, the rush of the pen to write the words faster. Is there an element of guilt in those written words?

Watch carefully, read those words carefully, decide for yourself. What are your thoughts? How you would react on viewing the letter before you?

The end was nigh. I'd had enough. Working hard and everything being dismissed. Coloured people talk about the past, the slave trade, but guess what? There exists the white slave too. Sometimes it is staring you in the face, sometimes it is so subtle it goes unnoticed.

On the 22nd November 2011, I gave up. I did not have the strength to leave the house, to face that daunting building and equally some of the low-life that I had the displeasure to work with. I called Janice at 8.09 A.M. and left a message that I would not be in work. Reason: that I was not feeling myself, anxious and stressed. At 8.20 A.M., I called again and told Janice I would not be going to work and confirmed my reason.

When stress kicks in, it is difficult to keep on explaining, to keep on trying to explain wrongdoings. Janice told me to advise her when I had made a doctor's appointment, which I duly did at 9.58 A.M. The appointment was made for Thursday, 24th November at 2.50 P.M., the earliest appointment I could get. Even now, as I write this, I am fighting back the tears. I never envisaged that my working life for an employer would end dramatically.

Janice contacted me again. She wanted to know what the reason for the stress was. I replied that it was work-related. She asked if she could expect me on

Wednesday, seeing that my appointment was not until Thursday. The answer was no. She said that she would send me a number for Lifematters Group within RB, which was sent to me on Wednesday, 23rd November.

I later read what was taking place back at the office to do with me. Janice sent an email to Garth Kelly asking for advice. The email read as follows:

Hi Garth,

Never got a chance to talk to you today as requested earlier.

Basically, Alice phoned in sick yesterday stating she is stressed which is work-related. As you know, Alice is currently on a 12-month written warning due to previous sickness levels. I have phoned HR to obtain advice regarding stopping her group sick pay, and her right to self-cert on the grounds of her written warning. HR have advised that this needs to be a manager's decision. I have asked if I do this can it be looked on as I am adding to her stress even though it states on her written warning that this can happen if any more sick leave is taken during her 12-month warning.

I am unsure what to do hence why I needed to speak to you to gain your advice. Can you please let me know what you think I should do?

Regards.

Janice did indeed speak to HR on Tuesday, 22nd November at 11.15 A.M. and was advised.

Why did Garth not look at the information on file? Did he have any doubts on the matter, given the fact that I had sent an email on the 8th August 2011?

His reply was:

My view is we have a clear warning on Alice's file. If she is not back to work within a day or two, then I don't see any reason why we shouldn't stop her sick pay as she has already exceeded the trigger levels in the first place to put her on a warning, so you have my support. If you want to chat through, just give me a call – I am on hol in the morning but on the mobile in the afternoon.

Regards.

The doctor asked me several questions about work, what, how and when. I was signed off for four weeks with stress. Janice phoned me later that day on my mobile at 5.10 P.M. I had missed the call as I was asleep. I wanted peace, I wanted to rest. I sent a text to Janice at 5.37 P.M. telling her that I would be sending in a doctor's note to cover for four weeks. The doctor's note was posted on the 26th November 2011 by special delivery.

Her return text message said that she had a few things to speak to me about and could I call her in the morning. I called her on the 25th. Janice advised me that she needed to arrange a home visit due to the reason for my sickness. It was agreed that we would meet on Wednesday, 30th November at 1.30 at the Wheatsheaf Pub, Coventry Road. No way did I want her near my home. I wanted my privacy.

Please, please leave me alone, I begged her in my head. I trembled when the phone would ring. I felt the pressure. I did not want to talk to her. She was part of the problem and she knew it.

29th November at 11.59 A.M.: *Janice, please cancel tomorrow's meeting and can we reschedule for next Wednesday, same time and place. Thank you. Alice.*

***

29th November at 12.12 P.M.: *Hi Alice, I really need to go ahead with our meeting tomorrow, is there a reason why you cannot make it? Thanks, Janice.*

***

29th November at 12.21 P.M. *Janice, I am on sick leave, so I want to wait until I can talk to you. Alice.*

Written warning or not, I was being intimated, my sickness was being dismissed, indifference crept in. Power was the ruler and the pushing continued. There was no rest, no time to think, to address the situation.

Janice left me a voicemail at 13:43 to advise that she was on a training course, hence the texting. My reply by text was 'thank you'. The meeting was arranged for Wednesday, 7th December, same time, and same place.

In February 2012, it also came to light that Janice had again spoken to HR at 11.10 A.M. on the 30th November regarding the fact that I had cancelled the meeting and the stoppage of my sick pay. Apparently, HR advised her that she called me about the stoppage of sick pay and the added advice to leave a voicemail informing me of this should I not answer the call!

Another voicemail was left at 11.18 A.M. on the 30th November. Janice wanted to really see me on the 29th? The meeting was originally arranged for the 30th. She wanted to inform me that in line with the twelve-month written warning that I received in June that the group sick pay would be stopped should any more instances occur. My pay was to be stopped from Tuesday, 22nd November 2011.

What more did she want? She was receiving the sick notes on time and sent by special delivery.

The day before the rescheduled meeting for the 7th December, I cancelled by text. I could not face it, that was the situation. I was human after all, not a robot with no feelings or a care in the world. Which reminds me, she once said to me that everything seemed like 'water off a duck's back'. No, everything was not like that, of course, I had feelings. There were tears, there was the hurt and the pain, the urge to run away from work, but for some reason, I hoped that things would work out all right in the end. But what was there to put right? I met the targets more often than not. I was liked by my peers, except those under the wings of certain management. With hindsight, I was good at what I did. I have the evidence to show anyone who asks.

A letter STRICTLY PRIVATE AND CONFIDENTIAL dated the 30th November 2011 arrived in the post. The letter was straight to the point, no humanity shown. Is this the normal practice for any employee on sick leave for work-related stress?

*As you are aware you have been absent from work since 22nd November 2011. Sick pay is provided at the discretion of the Group. As stated on your previous Written Warning issued to you on 2nd June 2011. **That any future absents may lead to loss of Group sick pay**. This letter is to inform you that as of the 22nd November 2011, your group sick pay will be stopped.*

I have tried calling you today the 30th November but had to leave you a voice message.

Your SSP1 form is sent out automatically after 28 weeks from the first day of absence, which will enable you to claim Employment Support Allowance through Job Centre Plus.

If you have any queries, please contact me to discuss.

Yours sincerely,
Janice.

I hated hearing my mobile phone ring. I hated the sound of her voice. Basically, I dreaded having anything to do with Janice. Facing her was a nightmare. I felt sick. I knew what she could do. There was indifference. There was a cruel culture from the top to the bottom of the business. As I say, I could not face her. I knew I would have to eventually, but not right now. I sent a text to her on the 6th December 2011 at 13.48 P.M. *Unable to meet tomorrow, not up to it yet. Alice.*

I had given up. Rules and regulations were just a smoke screen. As long as the business gave the impression that they were doing things correctly, then that was all that mattered. I continued to attend the doctor, who told me that I was making progress. He could see that I had determination and a strong character and that I would pull through. He would not advise me to go back to work. His point was that if I returned, I was returning to the same old aggression and bullying, with a strong possibility of being worse. And more than likely I would be off sick again just as quickly as I had returned. He was right in his thoughts. There was no going back now.

Of course, there was an element of sadness in how everything turned out, but that's life. But there had to be a light at the end of the tunnel. Maybe, just maybe, someone would have a heart, would want to do things right, would act as a qualified manager and display professionalism.

I could feel the blood being drained from my body. I turned pale and trembled as the phone rang. I could not answer it. She left a message, asking me to contact her by close of play on the 7th. If she was so concerned, why did she not do something about it when I was face to face with her in the office? Why did she condone and become part of the plotting and planning? Why the stupid set-up meetings?

I was being given no chance to recover. She wanted phone calls, she wanted meetings. Ever heard of letting a person recover? No, she knew the game was over and she did not like it. A quite aggressive letter arrived dated the 9th December 2011 by recorded delivery:

Dear Alice

I am concerned that you have not attended work since 22nd December 2011 due to work-related stress.

I have tried telephoning you on Wednesday, 7th December 2011, and left you a message for you to contact me by close of play Thursday, 8th December 2011 to discuss the reasons to why you have cancelled our two meetings.

I ask that you contact me immediately and by no later than Tuesday, 13th December 2011 so we can discuss the reasons for your absence and failure to comply with the group's sickness absence guidelines.

I understand that the details of your situation may be sensitive and I would therefore like to remind you of the service of Lifematters.

I look forward to hearing from you by Tuesday, 13th December 2011.

Yours sincerely,
Janice

Nowhere in the letter did she enquire how I was or hoped that I was making good progress and hoped to see me back at work, even that I was missed. No encouragement to step back inside the building, no attempt to make it feel good to go back to work.

In the meantime, I contacted the union representative on Monday, 5th December 2011. I wanted backing; my salary should not have been suspended. I was told to speak to another union representative, which I tried to do on the 15th. He was not available until the 16th. Even spoke to the Regional Secretary, all to no avail. I was told me it was a waste of time taking RB to court. They had expensive legal people who would make mincemeat of me! No matter how strong the case was.

The interesting aspect of all this was, when I phoned the Union office, a recorded voice gave two options, which were press one for employees, press two for RB employees.

I was instantly curious. I pressed option one and spoke to an advisor who asked a few questions and told me that no way should my salary have been suspended. *'Right,'* I thought, *'let's try option two.'* I spoke to an advisor for RB staff who said that it all depended on your manager if the salary was suspended or not. Such power in the wrong hands, but what was really shocking, why the difference in policy, or in fact employment law?

Suspension of salary is perhaps a difficult area; sick pay entitlement was part of my contract. Some sickness payment is at the employer's discretion, so they can refuse payment if they think that the absence is 'unjustified'. However, in doing so they must ensure that their decision is free from discrimination – in other words, not favouring one category of an employee over another when required not to. So, my contract was not adhered to. I was fully entitled to my salary as stated in my contract. I was faced with the reality that no one wanted to take responsibility for allowing the suspension.

I called Janice on the 13th, confirmed that I had received her letter and confirmed as stated in my text that I wanted to wait until I was able to talk to her. And a reminder that I was on sick leave. I promised to call her on Thursday to arrange a new time and date.

Apparently, Janice gave HR an update on the 13th.

I did call Janice on the 15th at 9.53 A.M. and advised her that I would have to wait until the next day, 16th, to speak with the union representative. Janice was on leave until Monday, 19th.

Janice phoned HR at 12.07 P.M., who I am told that HR told her to confirm that when she came to meet me that I had no rights to representation at this stage as it was an informal meeting to discuss what can be done to get me back to work and to find out what caused the stress.

In the meantime, I was being advised by HR that my salary should not have been suspended. Why? Because firstly, I had an excellent attendance record, secondly, I was on a permanent contract and had worked there for nine years.

I continued to submit doctor sick notes, always sent by recorded delivery and the postal receipts kept safely.

Yes, I did have an excellent attendance record. In eight years, I had taken thirty-three days. But I had hit the triggers, hit the target of four times, although it was only for nine days, then there was no mercy. Depending on your management, the salary was suspended. The number of days was immaterial. Guess I should have made a banquet out of the situation and had forty days off work sick. The outcome would have been the same: salary suspended. I did not have plans to take time off work sick – I wanted to work, but the tense atmosphere I could not continue to handle.

We read so much about how to deal with such conditions at work, how employers have a duty of care under the Health and Safety at Work law, put in place measures to control risks from work-related stress. It all sounds great, but in practice, it did not exist at RB. I could spend my time here relaying the moral and financial reasons for resolving such situations. Needless workplace stress is widespread in the UK working population and is not confined to particular sectors or high-risk jobs or industries.

Harassment/bullying – the legal term involves negative behaviour being targeted at an individual persistently over time. Negative behaviour includes the following: Ignoring or exclusion, giving unachievable tasks or 'setting you up to fail', spreading malicious rumours or gossip, giving meaningless tasks or unpleasant jobs, making belittling remarks, undermining integrity, withholding information deliberately, making you look stupid in public or undervaluing your contribution – not giving credit where it is due.

The Day the Eagle Had Landed

The day for the dreaded 'Informal Home Visit' came quick enough. The date, the 22nd December 2011, time 13:00 hours.

I arranged for a best friend to accompany me, Gina, but there was no way I was allowing anyone from the company into my home. As the saying goes, "An Englishman's home is his castle." I stated that we could meet at The Wheatsheaf, a Toby Inn, a very popular meeting place for business and pleasure.

I collected Gina in my car. Gina does not drive. I felt my stomach churn. For the next hour or so, I was going to be listening to nonsense. She was not going to help – she had the opportunity before and failed, besides she was the perpetrator.

I pulled into the parking space and Janice pulled alongside me. Gina asked if I was okay. I replied no. My mouth was drying up, but I must go to come back. It was something I had to do. It would soon be over, and I could go back to the safety and security of my home.

Claire Brown was with Janice. We got out of the cars at the same time. Neither Janice nor Claire spoke. Claire gave a little smile. They pulled back to let Gina and myself enter the building first. Inside we greeted each other, and the introductions were made. It was formal and gave the air of indifference to the point of passive-aggressive, one might say. We sat at a round table not far from the entrance. We were surrounded by people eating and chatting. The ambience was cosy, the lights on the Christmas trees twinkled. The open-hearth fire sent a warm glow. Gina took a notebook and pen from her bag, which is customary at meetings. Gina was aware of what I was up against.

The meeting began with Janice giving the reasons for the visit and explaining that she understood the absence to be stress-related. My health was not enquired about. On the table beside Janice was a Christmas advent calendar uncovering a chocolate for each day of December. On the top was an Oscar-type award, with a black base and a gold star at the top rising from a column.

Janice explained that this meeting was the third attempt to arrange, as the previous two meetings were cancelled due to me not feeling ready to meet. I handed over my new sickness note which signed me off until the 20ᵗʰ January 2012.

I was informed that HR had advised her to come and meet me to ascertain the symptoms and ask some HR-related questions. The questions were taken from a Google database, and were ridiculous questions. I do not remember them all now, but I remember two of the questions: Was I able to get out of bed in the mornings and was I able to wash and dress myself!

There was obviously no change – still the stupid questions, still the failure to resolve anything. Listening, yes, but indifferent. I reiterated my reasons for the absence from work. Janice asked what triggered the absence. My reply was, "I think I have said this all in the past." Janice stated that I had not said anything to her. I continued that everything had been said over the past couple of months and indeed years. She asked again. I have already said.

After seven minutes or so, it was recorded in the minutes Gina stopped the meeting and made a comment that this meeting felt more formal than informal and she did not feel comfortable continuing with the meeting and asked my opinion. I had to agree with her. I told her I felt like running. I was uncomfortable. I could see people at the other tables looking over. It was obvious there was no friendliness.

I did, however, state that my doctor had commented yesterday that he was not happy about the meeting as the sick note said the reason for not returning to work and that this meeting would add to the stress.

Janice continued to state that it was an informal meeting and that she was required to establish the reasons for the absence and to help with my return to work. She read out the questions to be asked, stupid questions. There were no signs of encouraging a return to work, there were no practical suggestions for returning to work.

After three minutes – I did not know everything was being timed – making, of course, the meeting formal, Gina, who was human resources trained, a fact not made known to them, stopped the meeting again on the grounds of formality. She did not feel that it was the right time to continue with the meeting and concluded that she was thinking of her friend's well-being. Gina took me to one side to discuss the case for dismissing the meeting, apparently for several minutes according to the minutes of the meeting, again making it a very formal meeting.

Upon our return to the table, Gina stated that we both wished to discontinue the meeting until we felt more comfortable and asked for the HR questions that Janice had. Therefore, we could prepare for the next meeting once we were aware of the questions. The questions were silly, not relevant to the case and made the business look like fools.

I told them that the sick note detailed my reason for my absence and that it should not take a meeting to explain this. Claire asked what made the meeting formal, that the meeting needed to be documented for HR and Alice's benefit. Gina responded, it was the HR asked questions that made it formal. There was no element of humanity in the meeting.

I was asked how I would like to be communicated with and what comments I would like to be passed to HR. I repeated myself again. The meeting was closed. Janice passed cards from colleagues to me and the award, awarded to me for being the person that staff went to for assistance. There was no mention of the reward in the meeting minutes. The fact was missed out deliberately. The final line of the minutes read, *After five minutes Janice and Claire left. Alice and Gina remained in the Wheatsheaf Pub.* That last line infuriated Gina. Firstly, it implied that we were drinking. Secondly, we stayed longer than was necessary. Well, neither of us drinks and there is such a thing as going to the 'ladies'. But then the business was particularly good at creating a smoke screen As Janice once said to me, if everything looked good, then that was all that mattered.

The minutes of the meeting were basic. Katie from HR had advised Janice to call me on the 28th December 2012 to say that she appreciated I had a sick note, but as a duty of care, I was to contact Janice on a weekly or two-weekly basis. No arrangement was made.

'Duty of Care' – it transpired they did not a have a clue what it really meant. The 'human' in human resources had taken on a new meaning. I was to discover it was solely about statistics and coming out on top.

Would Somebody Listen!

The reality was setting in. I was dealing with wild animals, people with no conscience and extraordinarily little management professionalism enough to listen. So eager to put a block on any reasonable discussion with me. Why? What were they afraid of? I wanted to find out.

By now, I was recovering, but my doctor was reluctant to let me return to work. And quite rightly too. There would have been no change. In fact, the chances are things would have been much worse. My view was if they did not care while I was on sick leave, then they surely would not be interested on my return.

I continued to submit my sickness certificates each month, on time and by recorded delivery, from the 24th November 2011, the last one being dated the 18th May 2012 for four weeks, taking the date due for the next one to the 12th June 2012. I spoke to various persons within the HR department. Each time I was told that my salary should not have been suspended. I also discovered that although I had sent my first sickness certificate to Janice on the 26th November 2011 to arrive on the 28th November 2011. Payroll did not receive it until the 6th December 2011. I was told that was probably the reason why my salary had been suspended.

There was no logical process in practice. Their own policies were sidelined. 'Obtaining any relevant documentation' – that was never an option. By the way, being a shareholder in RB did not carry any weight.

It is important that contact is maintained during an employee's period of absence, and you should agree on dates and times for this. During calls, you should: Ask about the individual's health, keep them informed with workplace information, and ask about likely return to work dates. If long-term absence, ask about rehabilitation and reasonable adjustments – contact HRAC for more guidance and assistance.

Employers have a duty under the Health and Safety law to assess and take measures to control risk from work-related stress. Also, under common law employers need to take reasonable care to ensure the health and safety of their employees.

How many employers do that effectively? How many employers know how to encourage a happy productive working environment? People spend many hours at work, so should it be a cause of discontentment. I am not suggesting that it is fun-fun all the way, but neither does it have to be torture.

Individuals placed in the wrong job, doing the wrong job, working with the wrong people, not cultivating talents and skills, allowing bullying, intimidation, job dissatisfaction and undermining the intelligence of staff. Allowing these traits to creep in only leads to increased sickness levels within a business. We have all read about the office culture within a major bank and the demise of Fred Goodwin, who obtained the title of 'Fred, the Shed' in the media.

ACAS, the employer advice helpline, beautifully worded advice with details on how to combat stress in the workplace by listening, understanding, and supporting employees to resolve any issues. They go on to add that 'some forms of stress can be prevented, the kind of organisational stress caused by poor management or lack of company policies for dealing with bullying and discipline'. I can assure you it is all good advice.

Now view things where there is no support, where there is a lack of knowledge and even more destroying the urge and excitement not to care, not to investigate properly, the failure to look at statistics to secure a good outcome.

I was tired, crying and stressed. Looking for someone to listen to me was hard. Surely it was not too much to ask. Apparently, it was. My head would hurt as I painstakingly looked up information and contacted HR requesting a meeting, for someone to take ownership of the case, but to no avail. Arrogance, arrogance was running through their veins, still, their demanding entitlement not to be beaten in their cruel decision to suspend my salary. I had family responsibilities and a home to run. That was no concern of theirs. My working life was ending in tatters. I had not imagined for a moment I was going to experience the nightmare. Years of working hard, proving all the time what I could do. The backlogs I dealt with; other people's incompetencies put right. All forgotten in an instance by people who did not want to listen. A few sentences could have made everything manageable.

I continued to explore avenues I could take. Checking government websites for information to help my case, checking out employment laws and contracts. All interesting and true statements of what to consider.

Direct.gov: Some sick pay schemes say that payments are 'at employers' discretion', which means that your employer can refuse payment if they think the absence is unjustified. However, in doing so they must ensure that their decision is free from discrimination (not favouring one category of employee over another when they are required not to). Surely, the employer would need evidence before making a drastic decision.

My contract stated clearly, I was entitled to sick pay, I was officially entitled to maximum 26 weeks' (6 months') pay, which was normal practice. If Group sick pay over a rolling 12-month period has been exhausted, the outcome of a formal disciplinary action taken because of sickness absence levels or where the employee fails to follow sickness absence reporting process then Group sick pay can be withheld or stopped.

Alright, let us explore further. On the 17th May 2012 at 9.00 A.M., I spoke to Joseph Church, Payroll, who revealed to me the following: Salary ceased on the 22nd November 2011. An online form was completed by Janice, stating her name and employee number – no signature. I was advised by Joseph that Janice would have sole authority for the stoppage of salary. She would require authorisation from her director, Garth Kelly. Garth made no mention of this fact in his letter dated the 31st December 2011 to me. Joseph also said that for a salary to cease other factors would have to be taken into consideration, which are the length of service and attendance record. And that each case is judged case by case. Hence my letter to Garth in December 2011 on the instructions of HR personnel.

As a point of interest, it has been noted that RB has been summoned to court several times for stoppage of employee salaries, the verdict by the courts as 'a breach of contract'.

Previously, I had written to Garth Kelly on the advice of a person in the HR department requesting a review of the situation. I was an employee for nine years and had only ten days sickness in the twelve-month period, therefore my salary should not have been suspended. I did not receive a reply.

By now, I knew that it was no use requesting backing or assistance from the union, so I decided to contact solicitors. The experience was earth-shattering, and only served to add to the stress and torment. I duly set about compiling the evidence I had, sending it off first-class in the post by recorded delivery. Or if the solicitor's office was near enough, I drove there and placed a large brown envelope into the hands of the receptionist. I was resting one afternoon, the phone rang. It was a solicitor with the words, "I cannot find the letter from HR, you did not put it in." Oh yes, I did, explaining where it was amongst the pile.

"Can I come and speak with you?" I asked.

Back came the reply, "I am sorry, but we do not see clients in person." Well, that was a new one for me!

That put paid to dealing with that firm of solicitors. It was a local company, Davies. What could I do? Nothing. I had no choice but to try and settle the issue on my own.

I grew in strength and made plans. There was no chance of me going back to RB. There was much talk now about redundancies and I hoped I had not lost out on that. I picked up on my idea of doing a diploma in career coaching, which I passed with merit. I explored the possibility of being my own boss, never to work for anyone again. I laid the foundations and got the opportunity of attending a seminar for 'Rights at Work'.

I arrived at the Grimscote Manor Hotel, Warwickshire where the lunchtime seminar was taking place. I had a mixture of feelings; confident on the outside, slightly vulnerable on the inside. I was greeted by the solicitor who was giving the talk, ushered into a room where other people had gathered busily chatting and was offered tea/coffee and biscuits. I began to relax and got chatting with two ladies, just a little polite conversation.

Finally, we were brought into a larger room with a screen for the PowerPoint presentation to be given. Different topics were covered. The most interesting one was discrimination in the workplace, how to recognise it and what to do about it. Interestingly, discrimination comes in two forms: associative or direct discrimination and perceptive discrimination.

Associative discrimination: direct discrimination against someone because they associate with another person who possesses one of the protected characteristics (types) of discrimination which are: age, disability, gender reassignment, race, religion and belief, sexual orientation, sex, maternity and pregnancy.

Perceptive discrimination: direct discrimination against an individual because others think they possess one of the protected characteristics listed in the above paragraph. Employees should always try to resolve a problem or dispute with their manager/employer first. This should be through the organisation's own grievance procedure. All well and good if it works well in resolving issues. Maybe, just maybe, an independent third party would be more beneficial.

I Wanted a Fair Chance

Yes, I wanted a fair chance for someone to listen to me, a fair chance for someone with a sense of moral ethics to view the evidence I had. Moral, a word I suspect most of them had never heard of or did not know what it meant.

I began to explore the possibility of taking a Civil Claim against RB, under the Health and Safety at Work Act or the Harassment Act 1997. After all, as my employer they had a duty of care for me.

I sent four pages of evidence on the 12th December 2011 to the Union Representative, to view. All I could ascertain was that the line manager had the final word regarding the payment of salary. Thick as thieves, as the saying goes, the union was never going to be on the opposite side of the fence to RB. I was fighting a losing battle to be listened to. I was hoping against hope that I would be given a fair chance. I have learnt more and more about RB since leaving the company. The culture, how even at the top things were not that good. One only must explore the internet and bookstores to obtain the information. The despicable behaviour of a person with an arrogant ego, who thought he was untouchable, and in a sense that person was untouchable. Never taken to task for the outcome. Still ended up in a comfortable lifestyle. I wonder how he feels now. Does he regret the loss of his wife and family? Does he regret the office culture that he introduced?

The 20th December 2010 was my first official attempt at obtaining justice and fair play.

We have received your letter that outlines your intention to raise a grievance.

***

This letter was followed by a letter dated the 7th January 2011:

I refer to your letter of the 13th December 2010 in which you invoke Stage 1 of the Group's Grievance procedure and now write to invite you to attend a meeting on 19th January 2011 at 15.30 at Brindleyplace.

***

13th January 2011, I received another letter:

...invite you to attend a meeting on 18th January 2011 at 2.00 P.M.

It is a long time to request to be listened to and evidence viewed in a fair manner and not one-sided. What was their problem?

***

I will fast forward to the 23rd December 2011. I sent a letter to Garth Kelly, which read:

I contacted the HR department on the 23rd December 2011 to obtain a copy of my contract of employment. On checking my sick record, the gentleman I spoke to instructed me to write directly to you as a matter of urgency to raise a formal grievance against Janice Duke...The gentleman was very perturbed by the actions Janice had taken.

The HR department are concerned that my salary had been stopped on the 22nd November 2011 by Janice Duke when it should not have been. Apparently, that action can only be taken when an employee's sickness reaches a certain level, in my case 130 days' sickness. I was advised that group policy would not have given such advice to Janice, as each case is assessed individually.

Also, I was told that I should not be on a disciplinary for sickness for 10 days in a twelve-month period nor should I be on an action plan for my work (details of which I gave to HR).

Currently, I am away from work due to work-related stress, details given to HR. This matter has caused further stress to myself and has had a knock-on effect on my family.

I would appreciate if you would thank the staff for Christmas cards received and for the nomination from fulfilment teams.

What the hell was their problem? A simple, straightforward meeting, looking at evidence, listening to both sides of the story. Then finally making an intelligent assessment and arriving at a decision. Not difficult, but if there is something to hide, then that is where the difficulty arises.

I was concerned for my well-being. Would I get into ill health? At times I thought my body would burst with the pressure I was under. Continuous letter-writing and repeating the facts repeatedly to solicitors, union representatives and human resources. I was not going to give up. I was determined to be listened to, but to the person that wanted to listen to me, mainly human resources.

I was aware by now that management at the office were not taking things seriously, it was play-acting to them. They were going to stick together, rightly or wrongly. Another letter dated 10th February 2012 inviting me to a meeting on Thursday, 15th February 2012 at 10.30 A.M. at the Holiday Inn, Birmingham with the Head of Customer Relations.

I was basically fed up. What was happening to me? Would anything be right again? I had to stay strong, I did not want to be beaten and to keep quiet to please them. I was eager to find out what was written on my personal file held by human resources.

I found out two things: that Janice had failed to submit my sickness note to human resources on time, which they say explained why my salary had been stopped, and secondly, that I had an argument with a colleague, and my line manager at the time had to intervene! What rubbish!

I was always professional, calm, cool and collected, ready to sort out issues at work, other people's discrepancies with customers. I had never gotten into arguments in the workplace. Sure, I was criticised for the tone of my voice, my ladylike appearance and manner. I was too cultured for a few. Attempts to make me swear failed and that fact irritated a few too. But that was who I was. What difference did it make anyway?

My reply to Jane's letter was:

Dear Jane,

Thank you for your letter dated the 10th February 2012. Since speaking with you on the 10th February 2012 I have received policy information from HR. Therefore, on the information received, I wish to cancel the meeting on Thursday, 16th February 2012 as I feel that the meeting would not be beneficial.

Yours sincerely.

Jane was a pleasant lady, middle-aged, and always came across as being all right. I never heard anything derogatory about her, nothing that I remember anyway.

***

20th February 2012, I sent another letter to Jane:

Dear Jane,

My letter dated the 13th February 2012 was to cancel the meeting based on the grounds that I have been provided with conflicting information by the human resources department. On their instructions and advice, I was told to write a letter to Garth Kelly, but to address the letter correctly to Garth B Kelly. This I did on the 23rd December 2011 and I received a reply from Garth on the 31st December 2011.

I phoned and spoke to Janice on the 22nd November 2011 to advise her that I would not be at work due to stress-related symptoms and that I would be attending the doctor.

I do not know if you are aware, but medical certificates have been forwarded to Janice. These have been sent via special delivery, with the exception of the second one issued, it was passed to Janice in person. The first certificate was sent on the 26th November 2011 and should have been received in the office on the 28th November 2011. According to human resources, they did not receive it until the 6th December 2011.

Further stress was caused to me when my salary ceased and gratefully, family and friends have supported me since.

Janice stated that she would be in touch with me, but unfortunately, no member of management has contacted me until I heard from Jon White on the 7th February 2012 regarding the redundancies.

I await with interest the findings of your investigations.

Yours sincerely.

I was concerned about my reputation, my character, my personality, and my work performance were all going to be taken away from me. This was a ridiculous situation. Human resources seemed to have two stories to tell. How was I going to uncover what was going on? I had an idea to go to the top and acted on the advice of a solicitor, who incidentally gave me incorrect advice on a compromise agreement.

***

The top man himself! Group Chief Executive of RB.

Dear

It is with regret that I must send you this letter, but I feel it is the only correct thing to do. Then you will be aware of the matter and will not be surprised if it goes to press. On the 2nd January 2003, I was appointed to the role of Senior Credit Controller, after a three-month probation period.

Needless to say, at the time I was delighted that I had secured a position at the company, and more importantly I was to be an employee of the Royal Bank, a major and important employer in the world.

Unfortunately, I have been subjected to intimidation and bullying within the business to the point that has caused me to be away from work with work-related stress. The attached information is only a scratch on the surface of what I have endured.

Recently, I have been advised by my solicitors, to request a compromise agreement as part of my voluntary redundancy package.

My solicitor will be contacting…to discuss.

Yours faithfully.

The Compromise Agreement

On the basis:

1. *I accepted my contract with…part of the Royal Bank Group, on the understanding that I could expect a standard of professionalism and Duty of Care within the company.*

However, the opposite proved to be the case. I was subjected to intimidation and bullying, a fact Senior Management and Board Members were made aware of.

2. *While away with stress, my line manager ceased paying my salary, contrary to the guidance of the human resources department and breach of contract.*

3. *Previous 'official' procedures followed as per group policy, but offered no long-term solutions, only heightened the intimidation and bullying.*
    a. *Informal Grievance*
    b. *Formal Grievance – which led to further intimidation and bullying.*
    c. *Disciplinary Action for Sickness – 10 days' sickness in 12 months due to stress brought on by bullying.*
    d. *Action Plan for Performance – Human resources advised should not be in place.*
    e. *'360' Feedback carried out incorrectly by my line manager and matter brought to the attention of my head of department, Mr Garth Kelly. I was horrified by its contents and the fact that I was being penalised as my partner had died suddenly. This was an element of the bullying process being carried out by my line manager.*
    f. *Formal Grievance, as instructed by human resources.*

4. *I understand from my investigations that the head of credit control department had instigated the intimidation towards me. The reason being I was a qualified manager, with quite substantial knowledge and experience combined with an impressive social status.*

I have always maintained a good rapport with staff, internal and external customers, coupled with loyalty and support for the business.

The Company have destroyed my good character, curbed my personality, denied my freedom of speech, the right to speak to my colleagues socially and to move about the office on business matters.

I can provide comprehensive evidence to support my statement.

I have applied for Voluntary Redundancy and in view of the environment in which I have had to work and endure for the past seven years, I request a compromise agreement.

I am willing to accept a realistic and sensible offer.

By this time, the letters were coming from various departments, getting nowhere fast or efficiently. There was no one who wanted to take real ownership of the case. It was a simple, straightforward exercise, made frustrating by the latter. But I struggled on, switching off as best I could. I was lucky I had good family and friends to support me. I even got to go on a few dates, nothing special. The dates only served the purpose of talking to a person who was not associated with my plight and therefore, would not spend the time together talking about work with me.

June contacted me with her findings. The letter was dated the 8th March 2012:

Dear Alice,

I write following your letter dated 20th February 2012 in which you explain the reasons for cancelling our formal Grievance Hearing meeting arranged for 16th February. Your letter provides further information regarding your grievance stating that you will await the findings of my investigations.

Unfortunately, as we have not been able to meet to discuss your issues in detail, I can only carry out my investigations based on the letters you have provided to Garth Kelly (dated 23rd December) and the one to myself detailed above.

I acknowledge that this process has taken longer than I had originally anticipated and apologise for any inconvenience that this has caused. I trust, however, that it will be apparent from this letter that I have spent a considerable amount of time investigating and responding to your concerns.

Please find below details of my investigation into your grievance.

My Role

As you are aware, I am the Head of Customer Relations and as such, I did not have any involvement with the issues surrounding your grievance. I am therefore independent and I have approached this grievance from an impartial perspective. I have also been supported by HR Policy and Advice Services.

Your Grievance

I understand by your letter of 23rd December 2012, your grievance related to your line manager, Janice, authorising the stopping of your group sick pay with effect from 22nd November 2011. Specifically, that you believe that Group human resources would not have advised her to do this based on your level of absence at the time. Also, you believe that you should not have a disciplinary record in place for your previous level of absence and you quoted in your letter 10 days in a twelve-month period.

In addition to your issues regarding absence, you raised that you felt you should not have been on an action contract in relation to your work performance and that you had provided details of this issue to Group HR.

Investigation Process

Your initial grievance letter was dated 23rd December 2011. Following this Garth Kelly wrote to you on the 30th December 2011 acknowledging your letter and confirming that you will be contacted regarding the Grievance process. There was a consideration as to who a suitable grievance hearer would be as I was subsequently appointed to undertake the role.

I then contacted you by phone on the 10th February 2012 and confirmed in writing that I had been appointed as your Grievance Hearer and inviting you to a formal grievance hearing on 16th February 2012. I received a letter from you dated 13th February 2012 stating that you had further discussions with Group HR and that you did not feel that our meeting would be beneficial. I then responded, explaining that it was unclear from your letter whether you wished to withdraw your grievance. Your letter in answer to this indicated that you wished me to continue with my investigations without a formal meeting taking place.

In order for me to complete my investigations, I have spoken to concerned persons and Group HR who have been advising me throughout this process and have reviewed the documentation relevant to the issues you have raised.

My Decision

I will take each point of your grievance in turn and confirm my findings and the rationale for arriving at my decision.

1. You believe that Disciplinary action should not have been taken regarding your level of absence.

I have reviewed all the documentation relative to this issue and can confirm that on 2nd June 2011 you attended a meeting that was convened under the Group's Disciplinary guidelines and the reason for the meeting was that your level of absence had exceeded the Group's policy trigger points. In that, you had taken absence due to sickness on 5 separate occasions, equating 10 10 days. The outcome of this meeting confirmed in writing to you by your line manager on the same day. You later raised an appeal against this decision, which was conducted by the head of strategic partnerships, who did not uphold your appeal based on the evidence concerning your sickness absence records. I have enclosed copies of the outcome letters for both disciplinary and your subsequent appeal to provide clarity regarding the process followed.

For clarity, you were issued with a written warning for failing to meet the acceptable levels of attendance following a breach of the group's short-term frequent absence triggers. I am satisfied that the correct policies and procedures were adhered to and can find nothing to suggest that the disciplinary decision or appeal decision were in any way flawed.

Therefore, based on the extensive investigation and appeal outcomes I do not uphold this area of your grievance.

2. You believe that your line manager, Janice, should not have stopped your Group Sick Pay on 22nd November 2011.

To carry out a full investigation into this area of your grievance I have reviewed the documentation from your Disciplinary meeting referred to above. The outcome letter, which I have enclosed, clearly states the following wording:

You should also be aware that during the period of the warning, future sickness absence may lead to loss of Group Sick Pay, the loss of the right to self-certify and bonuses/incentives may also be withheld.

As this written warning stays in force for a period of 12 months from the issue date, your subsequent period of absence in November would activate this action under the group's disciplinary policy for absence. My investigations have also shown that Janice did not make this decision before seeking advice from both her line manager and Group HR who both agreed that this action could be taken.

My thoughts are, yes, the action could have been taken but was it a fair decision for 10 days' sickness in 12 months? In my opinion, the answer was no, it was not. Was the doctor's certificate a false claim? If so, what made HR and Jane think that it was?

Back to the letter, based on this information, although I am conscious of the difficulties this action may have caused you, I am not able to uphold this area of your grievance.

However, in light of the fact that it is now some months since you have been able to attend work, I would like your agreement to involve the Occupational Health Team in order to fully assess your situation and provide you with any support you may be entitled to. I would be happy to initiate this process on your instruction.

3. **You believe that you should not have been placed on an Action Contract in relation to your performance.**

I have reviewed a number of documents regarding your performance throughout the relevant period of time and without the opportunity to discuss this in detail with you in a Hearing meeting can only base my decision on the evidence in hand.

There was an Action Contract put in place by your line manager on 11th November 2011. There were 3 key elements involved: processing of fines, RFT and Timekeeping, I contract clearly states the shortfalls against expected performance, and I have enclosed the document to provide clarity on the details involved.

There are notes relating to one of a number of meetings between yourself and Janice regarding these 3 areas which took place on 9th November 2011. I have enclosed a copy of these notes to assist you in remembering the meeting.

For clarity, at the time that the Action Contract was implemented, your performance stood at:

	September	October	November
Processing of Fines	63%	68%	55%
RFT (right first time)	88%	97%	98%

It is my understanding that you feel you are sufficiently trained and skilled to carry out the tasks of your role, both from the enclosed notes and your 'self-assessment' scoring on your skills and knowledge form which demonstrates that you do not have any training gaps.

Whilst I fully appreciate that you have no control over third parties external to your own team who can affect your processing time and to some degree you are dependent on the functionality of the photocopier, printer, etc. I have to conclude that each member of your team would be subject to the same outside influences on their ability to achieve target numbers and there is clear evidence that your own performance is not meeting that of your peers in the team. Therefore, I feel that your line manager behaved in line with group guidelines in putting in place a support mechanism to assist you to get to the required level of performance.

The third area contained in your Action Contract concerned timekeeping and detailed instances of lateness in arriving at work. I believe from my investigation that you were having difficulties in getting to work on time, firstly due to the timings of your trains and then later, your personal circumstances at home were impacting your ability to get to work at the required time. I understand that your line manager assisted here in agreeing to a period where your hours could be more flexible. However, it is expected that an employee attends work and is carrying out their tasks in a timely manner, irrespective of what that agreed time is. At 6, the time that the Action Contract was implemented there had been regular instances of lateness and the purpose of the Action Contract was to ensure that you understood that this was not acceptable and that it was expected to improve.

September	2 occasions
October	2 occasions
November	4 occasions (up to the 14th November)

The interesting fact is, no dates have been given, no explanations recorded for lateness...So, when exactly did this lateness occur?

The Group has a clear policy regarding timekeeping in order to ensure an open and fair environment for all employees. Therefore, I believe it is correct for any issues regarding timekeeping to be included in an employee's Action Contract.

Although I can appreciate that putting this Action Contract in place may have been difficult for you to accept, especially as you feel that you are fully capable of carrying out your role, I believe that it was done with the intention of developing your performance and cannot see any evidence that it was done with the intention to place you in a stressful situation. The purpose of an Action Contract, which is fully in line with group policy, is to ensure that the person concerned has all the resources to hand in order to reach the required performance and thereby improving the situation for both the Business and the individual employee and I believe this was the intention here.

Of course, no mention of the day I finished all my work. I had the final stage to do – photocopying the documents – the photocopier was broken, so I got a zero rating on my stats for the day! And that is fair management!

4. Level of contact from Line Management during your term of absence since 22nd November 2011.

In your latest letter to me, you stated that you have not had any contact from management throughout your period of absence until 7th February 2012. It is my understanding from conversations and reviewing your file that your line manager called you on the 7th December 2011 and left a message requesting that you call back. When no contact was made, she wrote to you on 12th December 2011 requesting that you contact her to discuss your circumstances as meetings had been cancelled. On 13th December 2011, you called Janice and confirmed the information you had sent by text stating that you were waiting until you felt better to talk. On 15th December 2011, you called to explain that your Union

Representative was on holiday and that you would call back to advise a time for a meeting. A meeting took place on 22nd December 2011 and it is clear from the minutes that you were not happy with the format of that meeting and that it was putting you under increased stress. As you raised this grievance shortly after this meeting took place, your line manager was aware that her contacting you to discuss your circumstances and a possible return to work was having a detrimental effect on your circumstances, therefore on the advice of HR, did not continue to call you directly. In the meantime, you had formally written to Garth Kelly regarding raising this grievance and it was then deemed that your line manager would allow the grievance process to be followed before contacting you again. From my conversations with your line manager, it is clear that your preferred method of communication has been by SMS text which she has continued to respect.

I am comfortable with the fact that your line manager has acted within group policy in that she made every attempt in the first weeks of your absence to remain in close contact. However, as you have stated clearly that your absence is closely associated with the actions of your line manager, it became apparent that any contact with her could have a detrimental effect on your recovery, and therefore, she has respected your wish to communicate by SMS text or in writing.

To summarise, whilst this may not be the outcome you would like, I would like to express my regret that you are feeling under pressure with regard to your work environment and would hope that we can resolve the situation as soon as possible and facilitate your return. To this end, I would once again ask that you consider the agreement to involve Occupational Health, as they could assist in assessing your situation and putting in place the relevant support for your situation. In addition, it is my recommendation that as an interim arrangement, an alternative manager now contacts you so that you are able to keep the Group up to date on your progress and to understand what, if any, steps can be taken to support you in your recovery and hopefully a return to work.

As stated, I enclose a copy of the following documents for your information.

- *Disciplinary Outcome letter dated 2nd June 2011*
- *Disciplinary Appeal Outcome letter dated 24th June 2011*
- *Copy of Action Contract signed on 14th November 2011*
- *Notes from home visit carried out on 22nd December 2011*
- *Notes from meeting dated 9th November 2011*

Whilst I appreciate that you may be disappointed with some of my findings, I hope that you are reassured that your line manager has not acted unreasonably or without Group policy and therefore, I am hopeful that we will soon be able to resolve any outstanding issues that you may have with the support of Occupational Health. I trust that this letter responds to all the points which you have raised in your letter, but if you are unhappy with my decision, you may raise an appeal under Stage 2 of the grievance policy. You should refer to the group's grievance policy for further information. Any appeal should be made to me in writing and within 14 calendar days of receipt of this letter.

Yours sincerely,
Grievance Hearer

***

13th March 2012

Dear

Thank you for your letter dated 8th March 2012, of which I received two copies, one being sent special delivery.

No doubt, you are aware I am a qualified manager and have knowledge of personnel matters. Therefore, I am disappointed with your letter because it is no more than a carbon copy of information already given to me by Janice.

Firstly, there has been a failure to discover the root cause of what has been taking place within Janice's team, and with Janice herself. On this element of the grievance, I will give you an insight into what was taking place and I will leave you to investigate further.

Janice's comment to Tim: It will be easier to get rid of you, but it would be harder to get rid of Alice as she has been here longer.

Janice's comment to me: 'What's wrong with you? Are you on drugs or been on the pop?' (When seen laughing with a colleague.)

Janice's comment to me: If I felt like you did, then I would leave.

I would suggest you speak with Garth Kelly, who can enlighten you about the occasion I spoke with him and told him I was fearful. Also, the email I sent to him on my return from holiday.

Work completed, but not counted as photocopying not done, due to problems with the photocopier, therefore unreasonable demands at times.

Secondly, I received a letter from Garth Kelly on the 31ˢᵗ December 2011 informing me that he would be in touch with me regarding the next stage of the grievance procedure. Garth Kelly did not state in that letter or indeed contact me to say that he had authorised stoppage of my salary. If he had done so, Garth Kelly, as Head of the Fulfilment Team and a Director on the Board, he would have informed me sooner and not waited until your letter dated the 8ᵗʰ March 2012. On that evidence alone, it would appear that Garth Kelly did not give his authorisation.

Thirdly, regarding the timekeeping issue – no dates or times given, therefore insufficient information. It is too late now for the details as it would not be true evidence. For my part, I remember being late three times: three minutes late, five minutes late and nine minutes late due to train delays by London Midland Trains. I would also like to raise the point that Janice did not speak with me at the time of the alleged lateness.

Currently, I am trying to come to terms with the fact that I went to work for as part of the RB Group, a major employer, and find myself in the situation I am in, as the able incidents I have mentioned are only a scratch on the surface.

I have previously taken an informal grievance, formal grievance and now a formal grievance on the advice of HR on the 23ʳᵈ December 2011. Management should not be placing me in such a position.

Yours sincerely.

***

12ᵗʰ March 2012

Dear Alice,

Thank you for your letter dated 22ⁿᵈ February 2012 which was sent to the CEO.

The CEO has subsequently passed your letter to me in which you have requested for your voluntary redundancy to be dealt with by way of a compromise agreement.

(I was instructed to send this request by the solicitors).

We considered that it would not be appropriate to respond to your letter until we had finalised and communicated all the requests for voluntary redundancy and voluntary early retirement, which has now been completed.

I understand that you have written a separate letter outlining the basis for your request for a compromise agreement and it will be responded directly.

I am also aware that you have sent a letter to Jane, dated 13th March 2012, in response to the Grievance Outcome letter you have recently received. We will deal with this letter through our Grievance Appeal Process.

I can confirm that following our acceptance for your voluntary redundancy request you will be contacted on Tuesday 10th April when formal notice of this acceptance will be confirmed.

Yours sincerely,
Director of Customer Services & Fulfilment.

So, there you go, I was heading for redundancy, but then so was everyone. I was delighted on one hand, saddened on the other. Yes, it was great I was never ever going to work there again, no more seeing the building that made me feel sick. No more trying to chat to people I no longer wished to speak to. No more getting the train, the train that took me to a living nightmare. Maybe that sounds a bit over the top, believe me, when you work with people with personal agendas it is a difficult time.

I mentioned I was saddened because I never envisaged that I would end my working days in such a trauma. Like most people, I saw myself retiring from the job and heading off into the sunset to enjoy whatever I could.

It was a ridiculous situation. It boiled down to adults refusing to listen to another adult. What were they afraid of? A solution could have been arrived at amicably. I began to explore not only what I was going to do workwise, but also how this matter could be resolved.

Determination, True Grit and Fair Play Required

I was on a quest for someone to listen and talk to me, to forget office politics and all that entailed. Maybe some people will regard me as naïve, others will see my point of view.

I had contacted various solicitors on the matter. Some were hesitant when they were informed, they would be dealing with RB. Others clearly only dealt with small businesses and felt that they could come out on top.

I contacted ACAS – that was an eye-opener. I mentioned earlier how their system worked – not good. I 'Googled' RB and discovered the large number of employees who had headed for the tribunal courts, to no avail. I wondered, as I read through the cases, what evidence was produced in court and torn to shreds, how many employees were torn to pieces by the experience. I did not want that scenario for myself. I wanted to keep my dignity, my character, and my personality.

I made plans for my future. All nicely taken care of, I wanted to be my own boss. I wanted to control my own destiny. I began my own business as a career coach. I had learnt a great deal over the years, coupled with the experience of management. I saw what can happen in the workplace, I saw how people progressed up the ladder, how staff were put against staff. I discovered that management in general can be blind to what is happening. Probably a mixture of being too busy and trusting middle management to do the right thing.

The tragedy is when it brings a business to its knees and destroys humanity in the process.

As I sit in comfort and peace tapping away on my laptop recalling the memories to write this book, I am pondering on how a person can go downhill from receiving postcards with messages of:

Alice, thank you for constantly trying to get the board up and running, keeping the team updated and getting the job done...well done and thank you, with *You're A Star* emblazoned across the front.

And

Thanks for submitting your manifest for the CEB, which I really enjoyed reading. It's great to know we have such committed, enthusiastic and passionate people in the business, and I look forward to working with you in 2010,

Alice, congratulations on Achiever of the Month, April, a beautiful lilac depicting a glass and a bottle of champagne, headed with *Congratulations.*

I was understanding from my investigations, I was told basically that the Head of Credit Control Department had instigated the intimidation towards me. I was too qualified, had quite substantial knowledge and experience, an impressive social status, and worst of all 'I could think on my feet', a trait that she disliked.

I enjoyed coaching my clients, from bringing a CV to life for everyone to shine with skills, character, and personality. The look of surprise on their faces when they discovered hidden talents and got the chance to learn how to view a workplace before stepping inside for an interview. They learned to have courage in their chosen profession and learnt how to be counted and when to move on to pastures new.

I started a weekly blog, and had quite a following, then I became a resident writer for a local magazine for a few years until I decided to try something new. I was delighted to be given the opportunity of going into schools and colleges doing presentations on work-related topics.

I persevered in trying to be listened to, amidst attending the doctor for new sickness certificates. I was making good progress, but the return to the workplace would have been disastrous. The doctor was convinced I would be back to see him again in a few weeks. Nothing was going to change at work, things would have been worse.

The solicitor sent a lengthy letter to the CEO. I will give a brief outline of the details:

Our client has instructed us to write to you in regard to a number of issues that have arisen during her employment with the company in an attempt to negotiate a suitable resolution of the same.

Despite senior management and board members being made aware of this, no action has been taken to prevent bullying. Our client raised informal and formal grievances about the conduct she was enduring, but the behaviour towards her continued from a number of people within the company at line management level.

Your internal human resources advisors have informed our client that she should be receiving company sick pay, but this has not been forthcoming, even after our client challenged this.

Our client informed management that her absence had been caused by the bullying and intimidation to which she was being subjected, but no account was taken of this.

Our client has always had a good rapport with staff and customers, and she has shown loyalty and support towards the company throughout her employment and therefore finds the behaviour to which she has been subjected even more upsetting.

We understand that our client has indicated that she is willing to accept voluntary redundancy from the company in order to remove herself from the unpleasant working environment in which she finds herself.

In the circumstances, we look forward to receiving your proposals in terms of our client's exit from the company and to resolve the above matters in the form of a compensation package, within 7 days of the date of this letter. Should an amicable resolution not be reached, our client reserves the right to take whatever action is necessary.

***

On the 23rd March 2012, a letter was sent to the solicitors from management.

I acknowledge receipt of your letter dated 19th March 2012 in relation to employee Ms A Kenny. I have referred this matter to our HR Policy & Advice department.

I must advise you that the Group has a policy of not entering into correspondence with Legal Representatives, particularly since internal procedures are currently ongoing.

I have copied this letter to your client, and I will ensure your client is contacted with regards to her outstanding grievance appeal.

Yours sincerely,
Director of Customer Services and Fulfilment

***

On the 10th February 2012 at 10.30 A.M., a meeting took place with management personnel regarding redundancy. I had a friend present.

20th March 2012, letter from the Head of Customer Relations:

Thank you for your letter dated 13th March in which you state you wish to raise a grievance appeal.

I hereby acknowledge receipt of your letter and confirm that you will be contacted in due course about the next steps in the process.

***

30th March 2012, a letter did follow, this time from another Grievance Appeal Hearer. It read:

Dear Alice,

I refer to your letter of 13th March in which you invoke Stage 2 of the Group's Grievance procedure and now write to invite you to attend a meeting on 3rd April 2012 at 8.45 A.M. at the Holiday Inn, Coventry Road. The meeting will also be attended by a notetaker.

The purpose of this meeting is to discuss the issues raised in your letter.

I have been identified as the Grievance Appeal Hearer as I am independent and impartial, having had no prior involvement with the issues raised in your grievance.

I remind you that you have the right to be presented under the Group's Grievance policy, either by a union representative or by a work colleague.

At the meeting, you will be given the opportunity to outline the issues relating to your grievance appeal and to bring forward any matters which you consider relevant.

You should refer to the Group's grievance policy for further information, which can be accessed on the Intranet under human resources.

Please confirm that you will be able to attend on the date and time stated.

Yours sincerely,
Grievance Appeal Hearer

I find the last statement remarkably interesting, *The service does not offer direct advice or opinion on specific concerns.* Well, I had been given advice over the phone by human resources by a few working in that department. So what was the deal? Surely, if everything is above board, everything should be acted out with integrity, then sound advice should be given. Or is there a plan, an agenda in not doing so? Let us be realistic. All evidence should be viewed, persons interviewed as necessary and studied on a case-by-case basis. It is not a case of black is black and white is white. It is more complex than that. Was there an element of not wanting to be beaten and to come out on top? Yes, certainly that was an element.

The letter arrived on the 3rd April 2012 regarding the redundancy:

Further to your previous meeting on 29th February 2012 (also held at the Holiday Inn) I write to confirm that you are requested to attend a further meeting to be held under the group's redundancy policy on 10th April 2012 at a convenient location.

The usual details about the opportunity to have a Seconded Representative to be present.

I attended the meeting on the date and the redundancy was set in motion, which I was pleased about. Nevertheless, I wanted a resolution and closure of the Grievance Hearing.

The 3rd April loomed large in my mind. Somehow, I felt there just might be a slight chance of succeeding in my quest for fair play. They say that you judge an individual by your own standards, having high standards, then you automatically expect the same from other people that you meet. Then you realise that not everyone has high standards, morals and principles as you do.

I wonder at times, how would I do if I sat as a Grievance Hearer dealing with a case? I know I would want to do the right thing, even if there was pressure from a higher authority to do differently. Why? Because that is my nature, my DNA, my heritage. Even if the answer is not what the person wants to hear, at least if there is an honest assessment and evidence, then that is proving fairness. And no one could hope for more than that – not even me.

I dare not be alone on the 3rd April 2012…

The 3rd of April Arrives

I certainly, did not want to be alone. Many thoughts entered my head, all vying for my attention and none really getting an airing.

Oh yes, I made sure I had someone on my side at the meeting.

We arrived at The Holiday Inn; the sun shone brightly through the large open-plan reception. We waited, my stomach churned. Was this the vital important moment when I was going to be listened to, evidence checked out? Well, we will see…

After some time, Pete walked in, the usual courteous comments were exchanged. Of course, there was the eagerness to enquire who had accompanied me for the meeting. I duly replied that it was a business contact who happened to be the managing director of his own successful company.

The original notetaker did not attend, in her place was Sonia, who I had worked with on leaving Credit Control. Pete made the apology for having not booked a private room due to the cost involved. An open-plan reception in a hotel is not the ideal place for private discussions, especially when comments are going to be damaging to corporate business.

Out came the A4 notebooks and pens and the meeting began. My support person gave an incredibly good explanation for the reasoning for the Grievance being brought. He also requested that my salary should without any doubt be reinstated. Pete remained silent. I could see clearly that he was out of his depth. It was apparent that he was blissfully unaware of what was permitted or not. He continued to listen to what was being told, but the meeting was flimsy on his part. Nothing was going to be corrected, yet a little urge inside of me hoped that Pete would investigate properly. He would come back and ask me for evidence, dates and times, names of persons involved, but no, nothing was asked of me. He said he had to leave the meeting as he had to be somewhere else, and that he would come back to us with the outcome in two weeks.

The weeks went by. I chased him on the matter. "Sorry for the delay, I will get back to you soon," was the rehearsed reply.

Six weeks passed and the reply arrived. I was annoyed and disgusted by the outcome. I had no case. Basically, the grievance was not upheld. I phoned Pete on the 16th May 2012 and told him how I felt. No wonder it took you eight weeks to respond, no doubt spending time on how to discredit the case. There was silence on the other end of the phone. No sign of defence was showing. I had hit the nail on the head. The attached Minutes were distorted, and incorrect details were written, spelling mistakes were splattered all over the document. Pete now decided to speak, telling me that it was the one I had signed. I certainly had not done so. Now he was clutching at straws. The only copy I had signed was the comprehensive Minutes written by my support person, who shall remain anonymous for my purpose.

It was plainly obvious that the facts on the attached Minutes were incorrect. Sonia had written that my complaint was about the incorrect form template had been used for the 360-Degree Feedback Action Form. What? No, it was about the bullying format/procedure that took place for me!

My salary was not going to be reinstated, even though it was a breach of the terms of my contract of employment. No investigation into why my sick certificate had been delayed by Janice, therefore not reached human resources on time. There was a load of probing questions to be asked and investigated.

I was annoyed but remained calm and continued to say what I wanted to say, professional always was my slogan. I proceeded to tell him that he was safeguarding his colleagues but let Alice go to hell, that was their motive. Silence. Nothing was said to this remark.

I told him that the matter was not investigated correctly, it should be for his part viewed without prejudice. Oh, the man spoke, only to tell me that he had dealt with the investigation thoroughly. It was clear for anyone to see that he had not. He had not spoken to those concerned. He quickly told me that Garth did not remember anything. How very convenient, or more truthfully, a 'cover-up' statement.

I advised him, "Sorry, Pete, but you will have to go back to the drawing board and investigate properly," as he had not done so. If management condoned the 360-Degree Feedback procedure, then it became a case for organisational bullying. I suggested that a person from human resources be present at the meeting and not reliant on just a phone conversation. Plus, human resources should not advise on medication or make medical judgements as 'not medically qualified'.

The phone conversation ended with no satisfaction on my side. Pete gave nothing away as to his thoughts, only giving cliché statements of no value to the case.

A letter followed dated 21st May 2012:

Dear Alice,

I write following our telephone conversation on 16th and 17th May 2012 and your subsequent email dated 18th May 2012.

As you are aware, the decision of the Grievance Appeal Hearer is final, and you were advised in my letter dated 11th May 2012 that there is no further right to appeal. However, I wish to respond to some concerns.

Firstly, with regards to the minutes following your Grievance Appeal Hearing, I am comfortable that they have been provided to you in an appropriate format. I had also reviewed the amended minutes that you had returned and have taken these into consideration when coming to my decision. Your amendments will be kept on file along with the original version.

During our meeting on 3rd April 2012, you had ample opportunity to put forward your grounds of appeal and provide me with any supporting material or evidence you wished for me to take into consideration when coming to my decision.

With regards to the stoppage of your salary, I am comfortable that this issue has already been covered in both your stage 1 and stage 2 grievances. Your circumstances were taken into consideration by your line manager, and with appropriate support from human resources, it was agreed that the stoppage of your salary was appropriate in line with the terms of your existing written warning.

In response to all other points you have raised, I am comfortable that they have been adequately investigated. Thorough interviews have been undertaken with appropriate parties and paperwork has been reviewed where necessary. You did send me some supporting documentation on 5th April 2012 in relation to 360-Degree Feedback which I have taken into consideration when coming to my decision. I felt no requirement to ask you for additional supporting evidence *since you had ample opportunity to provide this to me at any point during and after our meeting on 3rd April 2012.*

I wish to remind you that my decision is final.

Yours sincerely.

Well, that was that! It was easy to pass the buck back to me. At the end of the day, he was the Grievance Hearer. But did he really think that I was going to believe his cover-up because that was what it was.

At the meeting, my 'support' had supplied documentation and questions that needed to be answered or queried or even discussed. Most corporate businesses are extremely reluctant to want to listen. Why?

Here are the real facts.

1. Experienced hostilities, discrimination, and negative attitudes towards her, attempts to resolve these issues through informal discussions, but failed to bring about changes in behaviours.
2. Breach of the terms of her contract of employment and right to fair treatment when her pay was ceased without just cause from 22nd November 2011 whilst she has been on a leave of absence due to work-related stress.
3. Discriminatory and inappropriate behaviours from some colleagues which remained unchecked.

Required action.

A thorough investigation, validation, corrective action and an apology and adequate compensation for the pain, suffering and loss of earnings.

Over the period of her employment, Alice received various commendations from people outside her department but has not received any recognition from her own managers for her ideas and attempts to improve the department.

Alice has been subjected to unfair treatment when assessing performance against targets. Managers have failed to make reasonable account for Alice's unavailability, e.g. because she had been seconded to work in other departments and/or projects and/or been absent on annual leave.

Following her Grievance appeal in January 2011 she was subjected to an unfair disciplinary which was held on 2nd June 2011 and an unwarranted written warning. Alice was instructed to attend a disciplinary under 'failed to meet acceptable standards required by RB".

In fact, it is believed that the disciplinary was held in accordance with RB sickness absence – information policy, which states:

Frequent absence to mean no more than four occasions (of any length) or a total of 14 working days or more in any rolling 12-month period.

Where the frequency absence trigger point is exceeded then 'formal disciplinary warnings may be issued'…not will be!

Sick pay may be stopped and/or the right to self-certify may be removed for any absences that occur during the life of a disciplinary warning for attendance.

The line manager does not mention her reasons for taking this action which appears harsh, especially given the circumstances that Alice was on leave solely due to work-related stress (which was acknowledged in a letter dated 9th December 2011).

The notes of the disciplinary meeting record that a written warning was to be issued, but no record of an attempt to establish the cause of absence. Or if Alice were guilty of misconduct which would justify the written warning. No attempt to refer the matter to the company doctor was recorded.

The RB sickness absence – information policy does not require a written warning to be issued. On what grounds was the right to uphold the decision to issue a written warning? Did H investigate the circumstances and how did she determine that the line manager was acting in a fair and reasonable manner? What weighing did she give to the specific circumstances, i.e. this was the first time that the absence triggers had been reached in eight years; there was no suggestion that Alice was not ill whilst on sick leave.

The written warning has added considerably to the stress experienced by Alice and is directly linked to her absence since 22nd November 2011.

The line manager instigated a 360-Degree Feedback on Alice with another team member. The exercise was flawed because it (a) was only offered by one individual who is arguably biased against Alice and (b) was carried out without Alice's consent. As such it is a clear breach of Alice's right to 'Dignity at Work'.

The line manager held a joint meeting with Alice and Tim, whereby she stated, "It would be difficult to get rid of Alice because of her years' service, but that is not the case for you, Tim." Not appropriate management behaviour. Performance meetings should be with each individual and it is not appropriate to threaten employees with dismissal in such a manner. A clear breach of 'Dignity at Work'.

Comments were placed on 1-2-1 meeting notes:

'Attempts to undermine or attack the position of others' and 'is insensitive to the thoughts and feelings of colleagues'.

These issues were not discussed, nor was there any evidence provided at the meeting to support such allegations. The comments were sent via email to Alice after the meeting. As such, they appear to be retrospective to discredit and undermine Alice.

On 11th October, a 1-2-1 meeting was held by Janice, which appeared to have offered a positive feedback from the 'contact team for the number of calls taken', but Janice was 'curious…why some of the questions you could not answer'. Alice explained this was because of the volume of calls and the fact that she was part of a 'skeleton' staff whilst the rest of the office was enjoying an event at ProDrive in Warwick.

That was always the case, skirmishing for faults, twisting details to create a negative impression. The list appears endless. My thoughts continued to be mixed. I still wanted fair play, someone to recognise what had taken place. But then it was not a case to be dealt with by a coward, wimp or whatever description can be given to such a person. Yes, I realise they were watching their own backs, but they took on the role and title of 'managers' without really knowing the meaning of the role or the word 'manager'. Where was their inability to judge, see the details in the facts?

Being told by my support, "They did not like you," did not help me. There was no wrongdoing on my part, no violation of rules and regulations, no confrontations with colleagues. So, if someone did not like the colour of my hair, then what was I supposed to do? I am a practising Catholic. Someone did not like that, then give up on my beliefs to suit? Sorry, but no way. I had Irish connections, I was not going to give up on that, which was impossible. I was a British citizen, and that was a fact too.

There are no excuses in my book for degrading a person, destroying everything about that person. To what gain? I believe in live your life and achieve what you want in life, but do not destroy other people to get there. In the end, what did Janice obtain? What did Pete gain for not asking the right questions? Precisely nothing.

Demotion without justification; letter dated 6th December 2006, following a restructure, Alice was re-appointed to the position of senior credit controller but at a lower grade 3; she had been a senior credit controller at a higher grade 4.

Her salary was unaffected but eligibility for a company bonus was reduced. The reasoning behind the action was never explained. Was there a real restructure that affected the whole of the business? Who knows.

The report continued to mention the false comment held by human resources on their PeopleSoft system, which I mentioned earlier and was done without my knowledge or agreement. Plus, there was no reference to any evidence to support these serious allegations; 'failed to acknowledge complaint', 'offered poor customer service', and 'confrontational with a customer'.

Despite assurances that the latter note would be removed, it remains on PeopleSoft with a note that it is disputed.

Comments made directly to me went unchecked and unrecorded, comments which to an extent at the time I chose to ignore due to uneducated ignorance by the person saying them. It was only as events progressed that I thought more about the comments said to me. Why were they said in the first place? Basically, they amounted to ageism and sexism discrimination. Remarks were, "Are you a lesbian?" (because I was not married at the time), "When are you going to retire?" and "At your time of life you should not be thinking of getting on."

RB must only record information about Alice that it can prove to be factually correct, it cannot record hearsay, unproven allegations, or conjecture.

On reviewing everything, they had a plan, good, bad indifferent. There was clearly a breach of contract of employment and the right to fair treatment when my pay was ceased without just cause from the 22nd November 2011. That, my friends, appears to be the course of action RB adopts as a hidden policy.

Hindsight is a great factor, but sometimes it is of no help at all. I realise that now. *'I slipped up badly,'* I think. At the beginning of Grievance fiascos, the first one was my important step. Yes, I put a great case forward, but I made the terrible mistake of being trusting. I trusted people to do the right thing, to put a stop to the unbearable life I was living in those four walls.

In fact, the matter should have been dealt with under RB Dignity at Work procedure, but it was incorrectly handled by RB as a Grievance. The notes of the meeting are brief and do not provide any evidence that the allegations were probed by the Grievance Hearer. Retrospectively, I succumbed to suggestions to draw a line under the matter and to work with my current line manager. That was my crucial error; I succumbed to trust, instead of demanding without any excuses an apology and to gain the recognition I deserved.

The letter dated 25th January 2011 under the heading 'Decision' restates the allegations and records some of the matters discussed which are also contained within the notes of the meeting. However, there appears to be no affirmation or rejection of the allegations and as such there was no decision made. The letter incorrectly states that Alice agreed that the matter has now been resolved.

'Thick As Thieves' and Apparently Proud of It!

A nother letter arrived, dated 11th June 2012, relating to the Statutory Sick Pay:

According to our HR records you are, or to shortly become ineligible for Statutory Sick Pay due to an open absence being recorded on our HR records. Payroll has a legal obligation to send SSP1 form to every employee who will soon be absent due to sickness for 28 weeks regardless of the length of service.

Providing that you are still eligible for the Group Sick Pay and you have not been told by your line manager or HR that these payments will stop, there will be no reduction in your monthly gross pay as Statutory Sick Pay and Group Sick Pay are two separate elements. You will see the difference in your monthly gross pay only if your Group Sick Pay has already been stopped.

You may now be entitled to claim Employment Support Allowance. In order to be considered for those benefits, you will need to contact your local Jobcentre Plus. Details of how you should proceed with such a claim are explained on page 1 of the SSP1 form.

Eligibility for employment support allowance will be decided by the department for work and pensions and they will send you any monies that they award you directly.

Important

If you have not been absent from work recently, the absence recorded within our HR records may not have been closed by your line manager. Please speak to your line manager and arrange for the open absence to be closed as soon as possible. The letter and the enclosed SSP1 FORM can be destroyed and there will be no impact on your pay or HR records.

Yours sincerely,
HR Shared Services

Great! No pay, no sickness pay, but maybe Employment Support Allowance. Interesting! I was on long-term sickness leave. The rules for claiming Employment Support Allowance are you can usually work up to 16 hours a week and earn up to £140 a week. A person can only work more than 16 hours if the work is either voluntary or 'supported' permitted work.

Either way, the rules state that a person can earn no more than £140 a week.

I still had a legal binding contract with my employer, RB, and as stated in my contract, the right to be paid Group Sick Pay. I had not committed a major breach of my contract; I had, however, hit the 'trigger points'.

And on that point, RB used that factor to avoid making payments, not only to me but to other employees too. An employee could have reached the trigger points of 4 periods of sick, totalling 5 days, or reached the trigger points of 4 periods of sickness, totalling 50 days. The number of days, length of service, timekeeping were ignored.

Allowing such black and white rules saved the company money and allowed for unscrupulous 'bosses' to manipulate the system and individuals. Hence the fact that RB buried their heads in the sand and hoped that the issue would go away.

People moved on with their lives, but I wanted fair play, I wanted realism brought into the arena. All the rules and regulations, Dignity at Work, we do care attitude was only for show, to look good on the surface.

If they passionately believed in their rhetoric, then HR would have no problem in meeting with an employee to discuss an issue, looking at all the evidence in a formative, investigatory manner. My issue could have easily been reviewed as, I believe, so could other issues without ending up at a tribunal, a tribunal that no employee was going to win. Of course, this fact only strengthened RB's stance on dealing with grievances.

I was not going to give up. I became more determined to make someone accountable for listening to me. In essence to have the professionalism to deal with the issues. The next person I targeted was the man himself, the Chief Executive of the RB.

I received a reply from the human resources director, Group Functions & Non-Core, thanking me for my letter dated 6th June 2012 and my email dated 1st July 2012. The letter read:

I am concerned to read that you felt you had been bullied and that this resulted in you being off sick with your group sick pay being stopped. The Grievance policy is designed to support the resolution of complaints effectively and in a timely and sensitive manner. The persons appointed to the hearing of the case were chosen as they were impartial to the case and could look at your complaint objectively. They were supported by dedicated case consultants who reviewed all the investigation details throughout the process. (So, they did not discover the missing times, dates, and my daily task sheets, clearly showing the high targets I had met, did they?)

But then it was a rather predictable response.

I replied to the effect that I did not concur with the response and provided some examples. For example, the minutes of the meeting provided by Pete differed on a number of issues and suggest a closer comparison between the version provided by Pete with the corrected version provided by myself and my 'support' would prove this fact. Furthermore, it is not correct to suggest the differences were insignificant. As an example, the '360' degree review was a clear example of bullying by my manager. Pete's minutes incorrectly recorded that the wrong forms were used, which is not what was said. There were other examples where the minutes were simply wrong and suggested that the investigation was not thorough or impartial.

On the issue of pay being withdrawn, the point is that it has not been explained to me what reasons my manager had for (a) issuing a written warning, and (b) subsequently withdrawing my pay whilst I was on sick leave due to work-related stress.

Before issuing a written warning and subsequently withholding salary, a manager should act reasonably, stating the reasons, considering all relevant facts like previous excellent attendance records etc. for taking such measures. The notes of the disciplinary meeting provided to me did not record the manager's reasons for issuing the written warning and this, I believe, was an error in the process.

With regards to the sickness policy, do you consider that it is reasonable for the manager to simply take such action against me, simply on the grounds that my sickness absence breached the triggers on one occasion in how many years of working for the company?

I would like to point out that the triggers within the sickness policy are arbitrary but clearly designed to ensure that managers review sickness absence with employees on a regular basis, but they cannot be reasonably used on their own to justify the disciplinary action used against me. TO ISSUE A WRITTEN WARNING IN SUCH CIRCUMSTANCES IS BULLYING.

TO WITHDRAW PAY WHILST A PERSON IS OFF WORK DUE TO WORK-RELATED STRESS IS A CLEAR BREACH OF THE RIGHT TO BE DIGNIFIED AND FAIR TREATMENT.

All that I seek is a fair and reasonable treatment and I urge you to have the courage to investigate the matter impartially and thoroughly and put an end to this dreadful episode as soon as possible. But if the matter continues and the company continues to ignore the merits of my case then I will have to consider taking the matter further.

There ended my response to her letter and a waste of time on my part. There was no change to the decision and no questions were asked of me. Her words, "In her opinion, the matter was closed."

Another director, clearly refused to view the documentary evidence or to meet with me.

I wonder if she would have the same opinion if the roles were reversed. I doubt it very much.

I sent email after email to the HR Department, to no avail, and I was blatantly advised that if I continued to contact them, then an adverse comment would be placed on my file. Why? Because I wanted fair play?

Time went on and I had no contact from the HR Department or Occupational Health to enquire how I was progressing.

I made a phone call to Garth, director and head of department, to enquire why my salary was suspended. He told me that it would be in my best interests to terminate the call. Again, why? An employee's salary cannot be suspended at random with no discussion with the employee.

My mind wandered and thoughts came to the forefront of my mind. I was thinking over things that had been done and the remarks made. There was clearly age discrimination shown by the actions taken with individual staff over a certain age. Was there even racial discrimination? Had there been something written down somewhere stating some wrong that I had done when I had not?

I sent a letter. Gosh, I was getting tired of this writing, tediously repeating myself to solicitors and human resources. The solicitors feared rattling any cages, but they knew I had a good case, but at the same time, I was up against the big boys, as they say.

The letter this time was sent to Data Protection on the 10th September 2012 requesting data and copy emails that I had sent to Garth, an email sent to me regarding a Pro-Drive event and an email from Kiranne.

Unfortunately, that department was unable to trace the emails for me.

12th June 2012
The Final Day

The above date was my final date, the end of an era, the end of my working life for an employer. The very thoughts of searching for employment and facing and dealing with so-called managers made me feel weak. Of course, there are luckily great managers out there working hard for the good of the business and their staff.

Believe me, I had met some good ones, but unfortunately, when you meet the 'bad' ones it is hard to forget them.

Sixty emails backwards and forwards to the HR Department at RB served no purpose at all, only to upset me even more. Binge-eating on chocolate was my feel-good factor, that only served to add on the weight.

Mentally, it was an incredibly stressful time. Thankfully, I had a good family and friends to support me. I began to think what if I had not coped well? RB could have afforded the time but would not afford the time to listen to me. No, because their arrogance got in the way. They did not want to admit that things were not done right. The evidence was plain to see.

Is a person's life so unimportant to them? It seems so on a corporate level, but even on a basic human level, no one was interested? One director stood out in my mind. She appeared indifferent, uncaring, and so full of her own self-importance, clearly on a corporate level anyway.

A few books have been written in the last few years about RB and the office culture that existed. Many of the tales retold are unbelievable, surely 'food' for a good American soap opera.

To get behind the culture of differing discriminations, how did it all evolve, to begin with? Was it down to one person's prejudices, that person having so much power that their prejudices just snowballed? And then became the mire of office politics and discriminations.

The president of Ireland, Mr Michael D. Higgins, made a historic visit to Britain in April 2014. The Queen held a lavish banquet in his honour at Windsor Castle. At the banquet, Her Majesty the Queen spoke of the serious discrimination and prejudice faced by Irish immigrants in the UK over the years.

Was that the root of all evil? Racial discrimination of the Irish people? I thought back to the Irish people I had worked with, many of Irish descent. Were we to pay for all the wrongdoings over the hundreds of years?

The law states that employers have a Duty of Care towards their employees. How effective, I wonder, is that?

To listen to someone's voice is not difficult. All that is required is good hearing and patience. And at the end, if there are no winners then so be it. But at least the listening factor took place, and all was revealed.

I began a campaign, the want of a better word, for people to be listened to, and to halt the ridiculous discrimination of the Irish people based on history. Let us be honest here, the Irish country has quite a story of England's cruelty to the Irish over the centuries.

My Campaign Began in Earnest

M y letter-writing began again in earnest and I made the necessary phone calls. First on the list was Mr Ed Miliband. Three letters were sent to him. However, I eventually received a response, but not what I expected:

3rd May 2013

Mr Miliband has asked me to thank you for your recent letter and my apologies for the delay in replying.

I am sorry to hear of your situation, however, due to the parliamentary convention, it is appropriate that matters like this are dealt with by your local Member of Parliament. I would suggest contacting your local MP, who may be able to take up your case.

Thank you for contacting Mr Miliband.

Yours sincerely,

Office of the Leader of the Opposition.

***

As soon as I could I sent a reply, 7th May 2013:

Dear

Thank you for your letter dated the 3rd May 2013, which I read with dismay and bemusement. As a member of the Labour Party, the advice given to me does not seem logical. Because basically I am encouraged to liaise with an opposition party, who if successful in dealing with my case will result in a loss of votes for The Labour Party.

It appears that the response to my letter was given no constructive thought, as I have since been advised by a Labour candidate not to contact my local MP, of course for obvious reasons.

However, I hope that the situation will be treated as a serious matter, which it is. And resolved by those concerned as a matter of urgency.

Yours sincerely.

I did what was suggested to me and I contacted local MP. I had joined the Labour Party through meeting Jess Phillips at a local social event.

I was aiming and hoping that someone would take up the case. I did get an offer from John McDonald that he would willingly work with my local MP to investigate the case, this was not accepted.

My MP did indeed write to RB, but the reply was the usual standard and was passed to another person to respond. In essence, the case was closed and so ended that avenue.

The Prime Minister himself was next on my list. Now if he did not help, then I stood no chance.

I am writing on behalf of the Prime Minister to thank you for your recent correspondence.

Mr ………. is grateful for the time and trouble you have taken to get in touch.

***

17th June 2014

Because HM Treasury is best placed to respond to the matters you raise, he has asked me to forward your correspondence to the Department so that they may reply to your concerns directly.

Yours sincerely.

***

2nd July 2014, a lengthy letter from HM Treasury, but shortened here:

I was sorry to hear of the difficulties you are facing with your employment matter at RB…The UKFI's overarching objective is to protect and create value for the taxpayer as a shareholder, with due regard to financial stability and acting in a way that promotes competition. The Government is therefore unable to comment on these matters.

I would suggest you contact ACAS helpline which is the place to go for both employers and employees who are involved in an employment dispute. The Helpline provides clear, confidential, independent, and impartial advice to assist the caller in resolving issues in the workplace.

I wish you the best of luck with your employment matter and hope it resolves to your satisfaction.

I watched with interest His Royal Highness, who always adheres on the side of humanitarian issues, as my next port of call.

***

21st July 2014 from London.

His Royal Highness has asked me to thank you for your letter of 6th June in connection with your dispute with RB…

His Royal Highness is most grateful to you for taking the trouble to write to him as you did and he recognises the strength of your feelings about this matter, but I regret that he is unable to become personally involved.

I am so sorry to send you such a disappointing reply, but trust that you understand.

Thank you, once again, for writing to His Royal Highness, who has asked me to send you his very best wishes.

What a lovely letter to receive. It was heart-warming to read that my feelings had been understood. I was acknowledged as a human being for the first time in this sorrowful saga. I knew in my head that it was impossible for royalty to get involved, but I thought maybe something could enter a conversation somewhere sometime.

I decided rightly or wrongly to have another attempt at reaching the soul of RB, this time the new Chief Executive.

I got a reply, again my letter had been passed to someone else in the bank to answer my letter:

Thank you for your letter of 25th September 2014 addressed to our Chief Executive. To explain, I am responding on his behalf as senior manager within the Executive Office.

It is clear that this matter has been an ongoing source of distress for you and I am sorry if you felt that your complaint was not investigated thoroughly by his predecessor, We take any allegations of harassment and bullying extremely seriously and so I have reviewed all previous correspondence to ensure that I am aware of all the background to your complaint.

Following my review, I agree with the outcome expressed by management personnel, in their previous letters to you and your MP. I know that you disagree with this position, but I believe that the Bank has been consistent, fair, and thorough in our handling of your complaint.

Thank you for bringing this matter to my attention and I wish you all the best in your future career.

Yours sincerely,

The word 'closed' was etched in my mind. It was so final, the end of a story. It was the ultimate failure to want to meet face to face with me. That was the fly in the ointment to me. What was their problem? Was it so problematic to listen to what I had to say, to view the work logs that I had been keeping? To keep an open mind and deal with the matter with integrity? Show their skills and talents as senior managers and not cowards?

The final correspondence received 20th May 2015 from HM Treasury:

Thank you…I would like to apologise for the delay you have experienced in receiving a response to your letter…I am sorry that you feel that our previous responses have not answered your concerns. However, we have set out the Government's position clearly on the matters that you raise and there is nothing further that the Treasury can add. In these circumstances, we consider that our correspondence with you on this issue is closed.

And so the matter was 'closed' in their minds, and to an extent in mine too. After all, it is difficult at times to get people to listen.

Try to change a man against his will and he will be of the same opinion.

My Final Word

That is my story told, for better or for worse, but hopefully for the better. My reason for revealing the story is a simple one: I want the reader to envisage the scene, to understand the tension that such circumstances bring about. Not only within the individual but how it spreads to those close to them.

The tears that are shed in silence, the inevitable force of courage and dignity that is required to continue to stay in such an environment.

I realise that I am not alone. Bullying exists and goes on today around the world, in varying occupations and to varying degrees.

Many people survive, but unfortunately many are left traumatised by the 'torture' impacting their everyday lives by destroying confidence, wellbeing, and relationships with people they meet.

To bring to the attention of those with power and authority to understand the role they play in the workplace or indeed anywhere else. The role and title of manager means to manage the workforce with dignity and adherence to the needs of the business too. Both these factors go hand-in-hand for a successful business. It is impossible to separate these factors. Happy staff work better, they feel part of the business.

And as the cliché goes, "You can't do enough for a good manager." And how true that is.

Yes, many will argue that managers are humans too, of course, they are, but I strongly believe that prejudices and discrimination should be left at the kitchen table before they leave for the workplace.

Judge a person by their worth, their integrity and their ability and no errors can be made to regret.

I have no doubt that you are wondering how I survived, and the burning question of why I put up with the bullying.

There are a few factors that played in my mind. I hoped that good would overcome evil, which did not happen. I realised that the business was folding. There were many signs that pointed to that. Therefore redundancy was on the horizon and I certainly did not want to miss that opportunity. I had responsibilities to fulfil and could not face the prospect of job applications and interviews. Furthermore, I had proved my capabilities and my worth many times over and over. So enough was enough in my mind.

For my part, I have no bitterness for those who tried to destroy me. I would rather be in my shoes than in theirs. What did astound and annoy me was the attitude of the human resources department. It should have really been known as the people resources department. 'Human' did have a double meaning; people and humanity, but that has long gone. Maybe one day human resources department will mean that again.

I have moved on and made plans. I became a resident feature writer for a local magazine. Articles were all based on business practices. I furthered my management experience and qualifications and trained as a career coach and have my own business.

I thank God each day for giving me the strength, the ability and commitment to live my life and succeed in my ventures, both personally and professionally.

'Deceit is in the heart of those who devise evil,
but those who plan good have joy.'